✳ what you need to buy for baby

essentials

*what you need to buy for baby

essentials

caroline plaisted

foulsham
LONDON • NEW YORK • TORONTO • SYDNEY

foulsham

The Publishing House, Bennetts Close, Cippenham, Slough,
Berkshire, SL1 5AP, England

ISBN 0-572-02758-3

Printed in Great Britain by The Bath Press, Bath

Contents

Introduction

Congratulations! You are having a baby – one of the most exciting things that you will ever experience. And you've got nine months to prepare for the big event – lots of time to make plans and start 'nesting' for your baby's birth.

You've probably already been looking through the pregnancy magazines and catalogues, admiring all of the wonderful things there are for babies. But like most expectant mothers, you are probably feeling overwhelmed by quite how many things there are out there – and exactly what, when and where you should buy them! There's just so much choice, it's hard to know where to begin.

But that's just where this book comes in. Having a baby doesn't mean that the whole of your home has to start looking like a perfectly kitted out nursery. Nor does it mean that you have to spend a small fortune to get everything you need. Using the sections and essential tips in this book, you can make decisions about what you need to buy, what you need to borrow – and what you and your baby can live without!

Don't be influenced by all the hype: the advertising and direct mail promotions that start to come flooding through your letterbox the minute you register as pregnant, and the things that your friends and family tell you. By all means listen to and read what everyone has to say – and then use this book to work out what is best for you, your family – and, of course, your baby. It could save you a small fortune, will make your life easier – and save your sanity too!

Have a great pregnancy – and a beautiful baby.

> Rather than be inappropriate to half the readers by choosing to call the baby 'he' or 'she' – or using the clumsy 'he or she' all the time – we refer to the baby as 'he' and then 'she' in alternate chapters.

Chapter 1
Sensible Planning

Almost as soon as the good news has sunk in, we all spend many happy hours pouring through the baby catalogues and writing lists of what we want and feel sure we will need. But, despite being spurred on by both our hormones and our friends' best intentions, it's worth sitting back for a while before rushing out to the shops and buying everything at once.

- Using the other chapters in this book, make a list of the things you think you will need, then speak to your friends who have babies and ask if they have used all of them. If there is anything on your list that they haven't used, ask why and put that item on your 'B' list to think about.

- Have any of your relatives' babies grown out of any basic items? If they have, perhaps you can borrow these rather than buy new.

- Check out prices before you buy! You've got nine whole months to seek out the bargains, and to consider buying by mail order or via the internet to make sure that you get the best possible prices.

- Consider what equipment and clothes you will need for the first three months and plan to buy that before the baby is

born. After all, where are you going to keep a high-chair for the first seven months or so when the baby won't be able to use it?

- If you are lucky enough to be asked what you would like as a present from friends and family, be honest! 'Anything will do' may well result in being given yet another teddy-bear or your fifteenth newborn-size baby suit. 'Actually I need a yellow cot blanket' is more likely to get the result you want – and need!

If someone does give you an item that you already have or that's in the wrong colour, ask them if they mind you taking it back to the shop and exchanging it for another item. One good way not to offend people is to suggest that you already have another in the same size and would like to change it for the next size up!

Buying mail order and on-line

Buying this way can be convenient and cheap – as long as you follow the following simple rules.

- Make sure that any mail order is protected by MOPS (the Mail Order Protection Service).
- Use a credit card that offers insurance and protection of your goods and payment when ordering by both mail order and the internet.
- Check that the cheap price of the goods isn't being bumped up by an enormous delivery and packing charge.
- Can you give a second delivery address (such as a neighbour's) in case you won't be in when the package arrives?
- Check the average time that it takes to deliver the goods after they have been ordered.
- Make a note of any order number that is given to you by phone and make sure that any internet or faxed orders will be confirmed as received.

Some department stores and chain stores will offer special colours and patterns on fabrics for things like prams and cots that are not available either direct from the manufacturer or via internet and mail order suppliers. So make sure that what you are ordering is what you really want and have seen.

Buying second-hand

This can be a sensible and cost-effective way of budgeting for everything you need but only if you follow these wise precautions.

- It's best to buy from a second-hand source that you know (a friend or relative) so that you know if the equipment has been treated with respect and in the manner that it was intended to be used.

- Avoid anything when told 'you can order that missing bit from the shop' as you may end up with something that is now discontinued and therefore can't be used safely if not complete.

- Generally baby goods from a boot fair are a no-no. You have no idea of their history and no comeback if something goes wrong.

- There are lots of reputable second-hand shops and exchange shops selling basic clothes and equipment. Because the owners of these shops deal in the goods all the time, they will probably have checked the goods for safety and value. You can also go back if there is a problem.

> Never buy any baby item unless it comes with a BSI Kite Mark or an ECE standard conformity. Avoid second-hand car seats completely!

Family heirlooms

It's always good to be able to continue a family tradition or preserve a sense of history by using precious family items, particularly as another generation is arriving. But what do you do when your mother-in-law produces great-grandma's cot, complete with low sides, splintered edges and a dubious stain on the mattress? Here are some thoughts:

- A fresh coat of paint may transform the item.
- Find out if a new mattress and/or cover can be purchased or made.
- Take the item along to a local second-hand shop and ask if they think the item conforms to current safety standards.

> Some old cots and high-chairs may be coated with leaded paint. This should be avoided in all circumstances. Also, check that catches and hooks are safe and cannot be manipulated by your baby's inquisitive fingers.

- If it does, perhaps suggest that your mother-in-law keeps the item for use at her house when you and the baby visit.
- If necessary, be honest and tell your mother-in-law that, much as you would like to use the item, it really doesn't match up to current safety standards and you know that she would hate it if something went wrong and her new grandchild got hurt.

Chapter 2
Preparing Yourself and Your Body

40 weeks

An average pregnancy lasts 40 weeks and during that time there's a lot going on for you and your body. Here's a breakdown of what's going on inside you.

You should take a folic acid and iron supplement (available from chemists) from the moment that you try to get pregnant until about 12 weeks after conception. Ask your doctor or midwife for more advice about this.

Conception: This is calculated from the first day of your last period.

Week 6: The baby is about 6 mm/¼ in long and already floating in an amniotic sac. The baby develops from the head down.

Week 7: The baby is growing limb buds and has eyes and nostrils.

Week 8: The baby is now 2.5 cm/1 in long and has all the main organs in place, along with arms and legs.

Week 9: The skeleton is forming and replacing the original cartilage. The limbs are lengthening and elbows and knees are forming. The fingers have also separated. The placenta is developing to become the lifeline between you and your baby.

Week 10: Now the toes are separating and the baby's proportions make it look more human.

Week 11: The baby will start to exercise and is starting to suck – both things the baby will need for breathing and life after birth.

Week 12: The baby is now 9 cm/3½ in long but the sex organs are not yet externally visible.

Week 13: The fingers and toenails have developed but the baby has no layers of fat. The skin is transparent.

Week 14: The baby's heartbeat is now about twice as fast as an adult's.

Week 15: The placenta and the umbilical cord are now fully developed and providing the baby with nourishment from you.

Week 16: The baby will swallow small amounts of amniotic fluid that will pass through the kidneys to form urine.

Week 17: A fine covering of hair called lanugo is covering the baby's body to help keep the baby warm. Details like the eyebrows and lashes are developing.

Week 18: The baby may be sucking his thumb and you may begin to feel small kicks of movement.

Week 19: The baby continues to grow and get more active.

Week 20: The baby's skin is now forming into two separate layers. The muscle is increasing but the baby may still only weigh 340 g/12 oz.

Week 21: Halfway through the pregnancy the baby will probably be half the eventual birth length. But there is still no fat on the baby.

Week 22: Still growing, the baby is now more in proportion as the limbs will have adjusted to the size of the baby's body.

Week 23: Now the baby is 31 cm/12 in long with stronger muscles.

Week 24: The baby will have obvious periods of activity and rest. Loud noises may make the baby jump as the hearing develops.

Week 25: The baby's lungs are not mature enough to work on their own but the other vital organs function.

Week 26: The baby is getting bigger and even more active – probably making the most movements at times when you are resting.

Week 27: There's still no fat on the baby who is now about 36 cm/14 in long but fat deposits may now begin to be stored. The baby may open her eyes for the first time.

Week 28: The baby can recognise your voice now and her heart may beat faster in response to it.

Week 29: Now the baby is beginning to put on weight – possibly as much as 28 g/1 oz a day.

Week 30: By now the baby should be about 39 cm/16 in long and weigh about 1 kg/2 lb 4oz.

Every baby is different and your own baby's development may vary slightly from the plan above. Your doctor and midwife will keep track of your entire pregnancy to make sure that everything is going according to their expectations.

Week 31: The baby continues to put on weight ready for birth.

Week 32: The baby's lungs are now strong enough to breathe on their own.

Week 33: The baby can distinguish between light and dark.

Week 34: With the baby gaining more weight, she will be a tight squeeze inside your stomach. From this stage on, the baby may settle into a head-down position ready for birth.

Week 35: There's more weight being gained.

Week 36: Around now the baby's head may engage in your pelvis.

Week 37: The baby will begin to move into a birth position with the legs bent and arms folded across the chest where her chin is resting too.

Week 38: The baby may kick as much as space allows.

Week 39: The baby will probably be three times heavier than she was 12 weeks ago.

Week 40: The lanugo will probably be shed ready for birth as the baby is ready to be born.

What happens to you

Weeks 0–8

You can get home pregnancy testing kits that are accurate from the first day of your missed period. Follow the instructions for any such kit carefully, taking a second test if you are testing at a very early stage.

Book an appointment with your GP as soon as you have confirmed your pregnancy. Take a urine sample with you.

At the GP's appointment (often referred to as your Booking Appointment), you will be given an EDD (Estimated Date of Delivery) and an application form for Certificate FQW8 entitling you to free prescriptions and dental appointments during your pregnancy. At the appointment, ask what maternity services your health authority offers. Your GP will probably arrange for your first appointment with the midwife or hospital or give you a telephone number so that you can arrange this yourself.

> You may feel exhausted as your body begins to adapt to its pregnant state. Morning sickness could affect you but try to remember that it should all be over by about 14 weeks.

Visit your dentist to benefit from the free dental care you are offered for the duration of your pregnancy and for a full year after birth. Your gums will be particularly sensitive during pregnancy and your dentist will offer advice on how to care for them.

You are not obliged by law to tell your employer that you are pregnant but, if you work in conditions where you or your baby's health is at risk, your employer is legally obliged to find you a safer alternative.

Weeks 9–12

You will have your first appointment with the midwife. This is your chance to ask questions and discuss anything that you are uncertain or unhappy about. Take another urine sample with you (or go with a full bladder to give one at the clinic). You will be weighed, measured, have your blood pressure taken and may possibly have a blood test. The midwife will explain the midwifery services (including your choice of hospitals) offered by your health authority and set in motion the sequence of appointments that you will regularly have until your 40th week. The midwife will start a folder of antenatal notes that will be given to you. Keep these safely as you will need to take them to all antenatal appointments from now on.

At about 12 weeks you will have your first ultrasound scan at the hospital where you will give birth. You can stop taking folic acid supplements now.

> Your breasts may be larger and more tender and you may feel very emotional. At the end of this time, your bump may just begin to show.

Weeks 13–19
Find out about the antenatal classes available in your area and join the one of your choice. Keep up your antenatal appointments and continue to take regular exercise. Your morning sickness should stop by now and you may well look 'blooming' as you feel less tired. Your pregnancy will now be beginning to show so, if you haven't already, start to tell friends and family – be prepared for them wanting to share in your own delight as well as telling you their own pregnancy stories and experiences.

> The increasing bump in your stomach may mean that you
> go to the loo more often and perhaps need to eat smaller
> meals but more often. You may get indigestion and
> heartburn – ask your midwife for advice on how to cope
> with this. Start practising your pelvic floor exercises.

Weeks 20–28

This is the halfway stage. Make the most of resting when you
can but still keep taking exercise to keep you fit for the birth
and afterwards. Your midwife will probably discuss your birth
plan with you, but be prepared to change this as your
pregnancy develops and your feelings and needs change. Visit
the maternity unit of your hospital if you haven't already. You
may be given another scan during this period. Your waist will
have disappeared by now so you will need bigger clothes or a
few special maternity clothes. Get fitted for a maternity bra.

> If you suffer from cramps in your legs and feet in bed at
> night, try straightening your legs and flexing your feet as if
> you are trying to make your toes touch your knees.

You will need to give your employer your Mat B1 certificate
that will be given to you by your GP. This entitles you to your
maternity pay.

As your waist expands, you may want to use creams and oils to help the skin on your stomach to adjust and try to avoid stretch marks.

Weeks 29–35

From 28 weeks you will have more frequent maternity appointments. The earliest you can start your maternity leave is from 29 weeks but you will have to give three weeks' notice of starting it. By the end of this period you may want to pack your bag ready for the birth.

It's normal to feel apprehensive at this time, so discuss your feelings with your partner and your midwife. You may find that the skin on your stomach is itching – soothe this with cream but tell your doctor and midwife about it if it is excessively itchy. Braxton Hicks contractions may be experienced as your body prepares for labour.

Weeks 36–40

You will probably have weekly maternity appointments now and could well be feeling very tired. Your 'nesting' instincts will be at their greatest as you prepare emotionally and physically for birth.

You may not be able to reach your feet – so consider treating yourself to a pedicure. You may also find it uncomfortable in bed at night and need to support your body with extra cushions and pillows. But make the most of being able to rest before the actual birth.

What to have ready for the birth

Whether you are giving birth at home or at the hospital, you will need to have some things ready for both you and the baby.

> The maternity unit at your hospital will probably give you a list of the things that they expect you to provide for you and your baby – this varies depending on the health authority.

- 2 nightdresses – one for giving birth in and the other, with a front opening, to change into afterwards.
- Your birth plan to show the delivery team.
- Some water to drink.
- Music to listen to and maybe even something to read (although you may not have time or feel like it.)
- Socks in case your temperature fluctuates.
- Slippers to walk around in if you have an active labour.

- Money or a phone card as mobile phones won't be allowed in the hospital.
- Maternity clothes to return home in.
- A couple of maternity bras.
- Breastpads.
- Maternity sanitary pads.
- Cotton or disposable knickers.
- Toiletry bag with the things that make you feel your best.
- Newborn-size nappies.
- At least two Babygros or sleepsuits (some hospitals prefer babies to wear their own clothes whilst they are in the maternity unit).
- Cotton-wool.
- A shawl or all-in-one suit for your baby to travel home in.

> Make sure that you have a correctly fitted car seat in the car for your baby to travel home safely.

Go with the flow

Everyone has ideas about what they want for themselves and their baby and you should make the most of opportunities to discuss these options and choices with your midwife and the maternity unit at your hospital.

- Decide whether you would prefer a home birth or hospital delivery.

- Will your partner accompany you or do you prefer a friend's help or perhaps even want to go solo?
- Consider the pain relief options and be prepared to adapt these as your labour progresses.
- If you think you will want TENS pain relief, establish if your hospital or midwife can supply this or if you have to hire your own TENS machine.
- If you want a water birth, establish if you will need to book a pool and, if so, when.
- If you want your partner to cut the umbilical cord, ask the midwife about this beforehand.
- Discuss the policy on induction, episiotomy, the artificial breaking of your waters and caesarean sections.

Just as your emotions during pregnancy can be unpredictable, so can the birth and the way you feel about it. Plans that you made nine or even two months ago can seem unrealistic when you are actually in the process of giving birth. You may also develop complications that mean that certain procedures are no longer practical or even safe for you or your baby. Listen to the advice of your midwife and delivery team as well as your own emotions, and adapt to the progress of your pregnancy as calmly and safely as you can.

Chapter 3
Preparing Yourself and Your Family

The nine months of your pregnancy are a great time of excitement and anticipation of your new family life. It's a time when you and your partner will share many special experiences and emotions and perhaps, if this is your first baby, become closer than ever before. The birth of your baby brings a joy and excitement that cannot be surpassed. It also brings some sleepless nights and some devoted-to-baby hard work – and this can be a strain on the best of relationships. But some preparation and planning can help all of your family adjust to your new family life.

Preparing yourself

If this is your first baby, make the most of every opportunity you get during the nine months to pamper yourself and be pampered by other people. There's an old saying: Never stand when you can sit, never sit when you can lie. This may not always be practical and whilst you need to take regular exercise during your pregnancy to keep you fit for birth and beyond, you still need rest. Here are ideas to help you look after yourself.

- Take regular, gentle exercise throughout the nine months and afterwards if possible. Your GP and midwife can advise you about what is best and the most sensible for you.
- If you normally work out, inform your trainer or teacher as soon as you know you are pregnant. You can probably continue with most of the same routine but it may be wise to adapt some exercises or perhaps drop them until your baby is born.
- Find out about special antenatal exercise classes offered by your local leisure centre, swimming pool or hospital, and join up as soon as you can.
- Keep in touch with your friends. Make the most of opportunities to visit the cinema, go out for meals and have a good time out and about before your baby arrives and restricts outings.
- Find time to sit down and put your feet up with a good book or magazine, or perhaps to watch the television.
- Take care of your diet. The old saying that 'you are eating for two' is true in the sense that you need to avoid unpasteurised food and any other foods that your GP or midwife has advised you against. However, you don't need to eat double the quantity of food that you normally eat because you will just gain unnecessary weight.
- As your body grows and develops through your pregnancy, you may find that long, warm soaks in the bath are relaxing and help to ease away any aches and pains.

- If you can afford it, occasional massages and body-pampering treatments will make you feel great.

Some aromatherapy oils are not suitable for use during pregnancy. Always read the labels on products to ensure the safety of you and your baby. The same goes for any form of medication, whether traditional or complementary.

- You may not be able to see your feet towards the end of your pregnancy, so think about treating yourself to a pedicure; or ask to be given one as a present.
- Make time for you and your partner to be together. Whether it's a quiet night in or a trip to the pizza parlour, make the most of being with each other.
- Take a holiday if time and money permit. This could be the last chance you will have to be away on your own for some time.

Preparing your partner

It's impossible for your partner to experience the same hormonal and physical changes that you do during your pregnancy, but there are still things that he needs to adapt to and learn to accept.

- Share your joys, thoughts and fears with your partner throughout the nine months. You may discover that his worries are the same as yours and that he is just as vulnerable at times as you are.

- Encourage him to read the same pregnancy books and magazines that you do or explain to him the developments your baby is making during the pregnancy.
- Attend as many antenatal classes and appointments together as is possible.
- Discuss your birth plan with him and find out what his wishes for your delivery are as well. That way he can be truly supportive and proactive when the time comes.
- It's not obligatory for your partner to be with you during the birth. It may be what you would prefer (or perhaps it isn't), but it may be that he can't bear the thought of it. Discuss it with your partner and your midwife. Your midwife will have met many men who have been fantastic birth partners. She will also have come across a number who were not only useless but may even have been a hindrance in the delivery room. Take advice.
- Your partner is used to having you to himself. When your baby is born, he will have to share you with someone else for the first time. Find ways of showing him that you still love and care for him just the same as you always have.
- Once your baby is born, take time out together and separately. Make sure that you regularly spend time with just the two of you on your own as well as with friends (without your baby), but also try to make sure that you get the chance to go out with your girlfriends and that he gets to go out with his friends, too.

However much joy the birth of a baby can bring, the loss of the life you had together before your baby was born can be a shock for both of you. Sharing and talking things through with your partner can be a good way of coping with the change. It's not unheard of for both partners to experience the 'baby blues'. If this happens to you, talk it through with your health visitor and ask for advice about handling the situation. Whatever you do, don't ignore the situation and hope that it will go away.

The new mother sanity plan

Congratulations, you've got a new beautiful baby. And you feel exhausted … and your hair needs washing … and you'd like to sit down and fall asleep … Every new mother needs help with something.

- If you can afford it, consider hiring a cleaning lady to help you out for the first month at home. The responsibility of keeping the place clean will be a major thing that you won't need to think about. If you can't afford to pay someone, perhaps a good friend or relative could help.

- Make an appointment to have your hair done (get a hairdresser to come to you if you really don't think you can cope with going out) and ask a relative or friend to have your baby for you. An hour and a half on your own will make you feel fantastic.

- If you are breastfeeding, don't feel that you can't ever leave your baby because you don't know when they will need feeding. You can express some breast milk either for use later that day or you could even freeze it for up to three months. So your baby can still be fed while you are out.
- If you can't get the breastfeeding right straight away, don't panic. Speak to your midwife or breastfeeding counsellor – almost everyone gets there in the end.
- If you just can't get on with breastfeeding and have taken all the advice, talk it over again with your midwife or health visitor. Perhaps you could mix breastfeeding with bottle-feeds?
- Don't let your mother or mother-in-law make you feel guilty just because you do things a different way to the way she used to. If you are relaxed and your baby is well fed and contented, that's all that matters. Just politely tell them that you want to do it that way. If they still don't get the hint, ask your partner or friend to have a word with them to get them to back off.
- Have a good cry. If you feel lousy, crying and getting rid of all your pent-up emotions could be a good start to feeling better.
- If you think you have the baby blues, tell your midwife or health visitor. It is normal – and nothing to be ashamed of.
- Go out for an evening with your partner. But, if you feel that it would just be one pressure too many for you to cope with,

don't worry. Give it another week and then try to go out again.

You are not a bad mother just because you feel the need to have some time to yourself without your baby. Everyone needs time out and that goes for new mothers too. Don't feel that you are a failure if you need help to do some things that you used to do quickly and easily on your own. Every other mother is the same as you. You can't do everything – let your partner bath the baby, cook you supper, or whatever, whenever and as often as he can.

● Some health authorities make sure that all new mothers and their babies see a cranial osteopath before they leave hospital or very soon after the birth. If yours doesn't, ask your doctor if he or she can recommend one. An osteopath can help you to realign your body after the birth and may also be able to help your baby if they have been through a long labour.

Preparing your other children

If you already have other children, involve them in your pregnancy and new baby preparations as much as you can. All children will need reassurance that they will be loved just as much when the new baby is born. If your children are very young, it should help if you read stories with them that are about other mothers having babies. There are lots of great

books around with the same basic theme, either using people or animals to tell the story. Ask in your local children's library for advice on this.

You can also encourage young children to share the growth of your new baby with you. Let them feel the baby move inside you whenever you can, take them with you when you have your scans so that they can see their new sibling. Older children may also enjoy doing this but be careful because some older children will simply find it embarrassing and it could put them off. Instead, encourage older children to help you prepare the new baby's room or space. Get them involved with choosing any new nursery equipment or clothes that you need to buy. Remind them of stories about them when they were babies and, if you are going to be using prams and cots that they used, it will give you an opportunity of sharing with them the joy that they brought you when they were so young and did things for the first time.

If you feel your children are resenting the idea of a new sibling, you could try confronting an older child face on with the situation. Ask them what it is that they are unhappy about and why they feel that way. Always take every opportunity to remind them that your love for them will not be reduced – and that you will value the positive example that they will be setting their new sibling. If you are still concerned with the situation, discuss it with your midwife and health visitor.

Preparing your pets

If you have pets, you will need to take wise precautions before your baby is born. Even if you have other children, a pet may have got used to being the 'baby' of the family and could resent a new baby appearing in their set up. It's never wise to let your pet sleep on a human's bed and, if you have fallen into this habit, start making steps to stop it during the early months of your pregnancy. You should also discourage a pet from grazing on human food or being given titbits. How is your dog meant to know that the breadstick your toddler is dangling from the high-chair isn't for them?

Most pets can adapt to a new addition in the family if it is handled in the right way. But don't wait for a disaster to happen before you do something about it. Prepare your pet in good time – remember that routine is important to a pet: stick to a loving routine and your pet will probably be happy. If you realise though that your pet just can't cope with your new baby, it will be kinder to rehouse him before anything awful happens.

Once your baby is born, don't suddenly ignore your pet because that will guarantee jealousy and resentment from your pet. Just as you would with a child, reassure your pets that you still love and care for them. Don't neglect their routine – feed them at the same regular times and make sure that any dogs are walked just as they were before. A dog that is cooped up in the house all day and neglected will be frustrated – and they will take out their frustration on the incomer to their pack: your new baby. If you don't think that you will be able to cope with walking your dog, arrange for someone else to do it for you while you get back to having a more routine existence.

Remember that your health visitor and also your pet's vet will always give you advice on how to prevent problems.

It is dangerous for pregnant women to clean up cat litter. Ask your partner to do this during your pregnancy and always make sure that you wash your hands thoroughly after you have handled your cat (or indeed any other animal) and after you have fed your cat.

Your health visitor

Your midwife may introduce you to your health visitor before your baby is born but you may not get to meet her until after you are at home with your new baby and discharged from your midwife's care.

Your health visitor is there to care for your new baby and your whole family – including you and your partner. She will advise you on your baby's development, inoculations, and any concerns you may have about your baby. Working closely with your doctor, your health visitor will probably see you on a regular basis for at least the first 12 months of your baby's birth. She will help carry out development checks, basic hearing and sight tests – sometimes she will come to your home and at others she will see you at the baby clinic.

Your health visitor is not there to pass judgement on you and your family. She is there to help you and guide you. Think of her as a knowledgeable friend.

> If for some reason you don't get on with your midwife or health visitor, have a discreet word with your doctor. This could resolve any misunderstanding or it may be that you can change to a relationship with another midwife or health visitor.

Your babysitter

Even if you have a large and local family to depend upon, it's essential to have a babysitter (or better still a circle of babysitters) that you can call on to help you out. But don't find just anyone – you are going to be leaving your baby and perhaps other children with the babysitter so you need to feel confident that they can cope.

- Never use a babysitter under the age of 14 – it's illegal.
- It's best if your babysitter is at least 16.
- Take up references. If your babysitter is still at school or college, ring the establishment and ask them if they recommend the girl or boy as reliable and trustworthy. If the babysitter is older, still take up references: ask for the names and numbers of other people they sit for.
- Ask your friends about any babysitters they use. Make it clear that you don't want to pinch their babysitter but that you want to be able to call on someone reliable that they recommend.

- Look on the notice board at the health clinic or baby clinic for names and numbers of people who are looking for work as sitters.
- Ask at the local college for the names of students who are studying for a nursery care course.
- Find a local granny. Again, use your networking skills to find out about any local ladies who perhaps love children but whose own have grown up – or perhaps live too far away.
- Establish what the going rate is for babysitters from your friends. The price varies depending on their area that you live in and will almost certainly go up after 11 o'clock up night.
- When you book a sitter, clarify the rate you will be paying and what time you expect them to arrive.
- Try to give a sitter an idea of the time you intend to be home – and try to stick to it.
- Give your sitter a number that they can contact you on when you are out.
- You should also give your sitter the telephone number of your doctor and perhaps a neighbour, too.
- Establish the ground rules of your home. Tell them what you won't tolerate (smoking, loud music, surfing the net from your computer, phoning their mates, bringing boyfriends with them, or whatever you won't put up with) and make sure that you stick with it. If they break your rules, warn them or don't use them again.

- Establish how your babysitter is going to get home. It is unreasonable to expect a young babysitter to walk home on their own if it is late at night, even if they live round the corner.
- Trust your instincts. If you feel unhappy about a babysitter, don't use them.

Chapter 4
Preparing Your Home

Everyone has their own ideas and preferences when it comes to where their newborn is going to spend its first few nights or weeks. But you will still need to find a place to keep your baby's paraphernalia and also need to decide where the baby will sleep when she is older. You may have no choice when it comes to the room that will be the 'nursery', but you still need to consider the following points.

- Does the room have a door so that the baby can have privacy from the rest of the family?
- Is the room warm in the winter and cool in the summer?

Get a good nursery thermometer and place it in a central place in the baby's room. Keep it away from the radiator and free from draughts so that you can get an accurate reading. It is essential to ensure that your baby is sleeping in the right conditions all year round.

- Is there room for a cot?
- Can the cot be positioned away from the radiator?
- Does the radiator have a self-thermostat?
- Is there a window?

- Can the window be opened and closed?
- Have window locks been fitted?
- If the window is close to the position for the cot, will the baby be able to pull up on to the windowsill once she learns to stand?
- Do you need to fix safety bars to the window?
- Will the curtains keep out the daylight during a daytime nap?
- Is there a space for a chair for you to sit when night-feeding?
- Where can you keep the changing mat or changing unit?
- Is there an electrical socket for a nightlight and a baby monitor?
- Where will you keep clothes and nappies?
- Is there a smoke alarm in or near the room?

You will find more about cots and bedding on page 58. For information about changing equipment, see page 92. Health and safety advice is given on page 164.

Your baby and the kitchen

You have no idea how neat and tidy your house is until your baby arrives. Suddenly it isn't any more. Tiny bundles of joy that they are, babies seem to acquire so many possessions that you will find them all over the house if you aren't careful. A little forward planning will help.

- Clear space in a kitchen cabinet for storing powdered milk, sterilising solutions, empty feeding bottles and teats, bowls and spoons.

- Work out the best place to keep the sterilising unit, both in and out of use.
- If you are going to use a microwave steriliser, measure the inside of your microwave before you buy to make sure the sterilising unit will fit inside the cavity and has space to turn round on the turntable.
- Is there space in the kitchen to store the high-chair when it's not in use?
- If you are going to bottle-feed, do you have space in the fridge to store prepared bottles? If not, consider a replacement and start budgeting now.

> If you are replacing any of your electrical kitchen appliances, select items that are already fitted with curly flexes and have 'cool to touch' surfaces.

- Fit fridge, cooker, and cabinet safety catches or locks.
- Are all flexes out of a toddler's reach?
- Fit the kettle with a curly flex if it doesn't already have one.
- Where will you keep a hot iron when it is no longer being used?
- Buy plenty of paper kitchen towels and disinfectant spray or wipes for cleaning surfaces.

Don't forget to check out the Health and Safety advice on page 164.

Coping with the laundry

Washing is always part of everyday life but be prepared to increase the amount of time that you use your washing-machine and ironing-board once your baby arrives.

● Can your current washing-machine cope with the increased workload? If not, start budgeting now to replace it.

● Where will you dry your washing in damp weather or if you live in a flat?

● Buy an old-fashioned clothes'-horse that can be folded flat when not in use.

● If you have an outdoor washing-line, consider ways in which you can add a second line to increase the hanging space.

Check out the sales for bargain prices when replacing your washing-machine or buying a tumble-dryer. You should also ask how energy efficient the appliance is.

● Do you have a tumble-dryer? If not, do you have space for one? (Don't forget to consider the running costs of one as many can be hungry on electricity. You also need to consider air circulation for a dryer.)

- Consider now where you will store washing-powders and detergents. Keep them away from floors and out of a toddler's reach.
- Start storing both the ironing-board and the iron well out of a toddler's grabbing power. You should consider fitting a rack that will hold both of them in position so that they can't topple on to an inquisitive infant.

Electrical safety and smoke alarms

There is a lot more information about health and safety on page 164, but walk around your home and consider the following important aspects.

- Fit out your home with smoke alarms following the guidance of your local fire brigade.
- Regularly check that the batteries in smoke alarms are in working order.
- Buy flex-tidyers that will keep groups of electric cables together and under control.
- Never overload an electrical socket.
- If you supplement your heating with electric bar heaters, position them so that they are not a potential trip hazard.

Get down on your hands and knees to examine your home from a baby's angle. You may only spot some of the hazards once you see things from this point of view.

Chapter 5
Clothes

Many hospitals prefer babies to use hospital gowns while they remain within the hospital's care. This saves the confusion of clothes being lost or placed into the hospital laundry. Even so, you will still need some clothes for your baby to come home in, as well as the clothes that you want your baby to wear for the first few weeks or months.

Everyday clothes for your baby

It's hard to know exactly what size to buy for your baby until he is actually born and you know his weight and length. Even so, you will need some clothes for your baby to wear and it's therefore a good idea to buy at least a basic wardrobe of newborn-size clothes to have ready for use.

Babies can need frequent changes of clothes, so allowing for time to do the washing and then the drying and ironing of clothes, you will need at least five of the following basic items.

- Vests or bodysuits that are popper closed underneath the baby's nappy
- All-in-one sleepsuits (ones which popper up at the front are probably easiest for you to use)

- Bibs
- Muslin squares

And two each of the following:
- Scratch mitts (if you decide to use them)
- Booties
- Mittens (if it's the winter)
- Hats
- Cardigans (lighter-weight ones for summer babies)

And one each of the following:
- Outdoor all-in-one
- Shawl or smaller lighter-weight blanket

> If your baby is premature or simply very small, you may
> need to buy special premature baby clothing. This is
> available from many chain stores or ask your hospital or
> midwife for help in tracking some down. Don't buy too
> much, though, as your baby will soon outgrow them.

The above is a basic list of clothes that should be sufficient to
keep your baby warm and clean-clothed, but you are bound to
be given more clothes or see other clothes (like little dresses and
matching two-piece suits) that catch your eye and will look
gorgeous on your baby. When you are choosing clothes for
your baby, remember the following tips.
- Everything must be machine washable.
- You may also want everything to be suitable for tumble-
  drying.
- Clothes that do up at the front are usually easier to cope with
  on a newborn baby.
- Avoid clothes that may leave a draughty gap around your
  baby's tummy.
- Clothes that can popper undone around the legs and bottom
  will make nappy changing much easier (and warmer for your
  baby).

- Outfits with lacy and frilly collars may be irritating to your baby's delicate skin.
- Ensure that the clothes will be big enough to cope with the size of the nappy around the bottom area.
- Outfits with lots of fiddly buttons and hooks could be more hassle than you have time to cope with.

> Pure cotton or high-cotton content clothing may be more suitable for a baby's delicate skin.

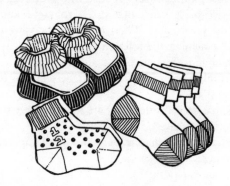

Non-essential items
There are so many gorgeous clothes to choose from for babies
that you may be tempted by other items. Keep your priorities
and the season in mind. There's no point buying a coat for a
six-month-old if your baby will be that age in the height of
summer.
- A coat
- Dungarees
- Dresses with matching bloomers
- Pram shoes or boots
- Tights and socks

> Always wash your baby's clothes in a non-biological
> washing-powder to avoid irritating your baby's skin.

What to take to hospital for your baby
You may only be in hospital for a very short time, so have the
following items ready for your baby's journey home.
- Vest or body suit
- Sleepsuit
- Couple of muslin squares
- Blanket or shawl
- Pair of scratch mitts
- Hat
- Outdoor all-in-one
- Car seat

Unless a car seat is fitted correctly, it will not offer the safety that is essential to your baby. Always fit a car seat according to the manufacturer's instructions. NEVER save time or effort when putting your baby and their car seat into any vehicle.

What clothes next?

You will be surprised how quickly your baby grows out of their first clothes. Don't worry if your baby is larger or smaller than the sizes indicated on labels for age ranges. Manufacturers' sizes tend to vary and you should remember that the sizes given are only guides. Your health visitor or GP will tell you if your baby's weight is not satisfactory.

Don't feel obliged to dress your baby in an outfit that you don't like or that is a duplicate of another just because it is a gift. Thank the donor and ask them if they mind if you change it for another larger one or another item because you 'already have so many clothes for this age'. It is better to be honest than either waste the item or disappoint the giver because they will never see your baby wearing the item.

After a few weeks of changing your baby, you will soon get a feel of the type of clothes that you prefer your baby to wear. If you prefer to continue with simple sleepsuits during the day, then that's fine. Similarly, you may prefer your baby to progress to dresses or dungarees at an early stage – and that's also fine. Always choose and do what feels best for you and your baby.

Always dress your baby in clothes that are big enough – particularly all-in-one outfits and sleepsuits. Your baby's legs and feet need plenty of space to move and allow growth. When a sleepsuit is too small, it will not only be snug around the body but your baby's toes will turn back at the ends.

Chapter 6
Sleeping

I t will take a while for you and your baby to fall into a routine of sleeping, feeding and waking at times that fall in more naturally with the general routine of your home. Some babies do this after a few months, others may take up to a year. But having a comfortable and peaceful place for your baby to sleep will help to make her (and you) feel relaxed and more inclined to rest.

As your baby grows, she will need different types of bedding to accommodate her changing size, mobility and comfort.

Cradles and Moses baskets

A newborn baby needs the comfort and security of a smaller cradle or Moses basket to sleep in. What you choose is personal preference so here are some ideas that will help you to make a decision:

Moses baskets

- Usually made of soft and natural palm leaf, you can buy them complete with a covered mattress.
- You can make covers to decorate the basket to match your nursery décor or buy them with stylish, washable linen.

- They have handles that make them portable for when your baby needs to be moved but you don't want to wake her.
- Many Moses baskets come complete with a hood which can add privacy or shade from the sun or draughts.

- A Moses basket can be safely placed in the middle of a double bed or positioned on the floor (as long as it is away from draughts and animals).
- Special stands are available to support the Moses basket. These can be folded away when not in use or for travel.
- Moses baskets can be bought very cheaply – although the more fancy the linen, the more you will pay.
- A Moses basket is ideal for your baby's first few weeks when you may wish to have the Moses basket next to your own bed for night-time feeds.

Although a sleeping baby can be easily moved around in a Moses basket, never allow your baby to travel in one in a car.

Cradles and cribs

These are a very traditional bed for a new-born baby to sleep in. Usually made from wood, they are much smaller than cots designed for older babies and toddlers.

Although they can look beautiful, bear in mind the cost of buying a traditional cradle or crib. They are often not much cheaper than the price of a full-size cot that your baby will need after a few months anyway.

- Most cradles and cribs have a rocking facility which can help to soothe some babies.
- New cradles and cribs come with locking devices that make it easier for you when you are placing or removing your baby.
- They can look gorgeous as they can be decorated with drapes as well as co-ordinated linen.

> Your pram may come with a removable body or carrycot. Although this will be quite heavy and bulky, you could consider using this as your baby's bed for the first few months.

Cots

Once you have established your night-time routine and your baby is larger, you may wish to move your baby to her own room and a larger cot. There is an enormous variety of cots available and prices start at reasonable and go up to very expensive. Look for the following requirements when choosing a cot.

- The cot should have one side which drops down to make access to and from the cot with your baby easy. Test as many cots as you can to ensure that you will be able to drop the side easily using only one hand and perhaps one foot. (Don't be embarrassed to hold a large teddy-bear in your other hand while you do this.)

- A two-position mattress base will mean the cot can adapt and be safe as your baby becomes more mobile. The higher position will suit a younger baby but once your baby learns to roll and definitely when she learns to sit and pull herself up, you will need a lower position for the mattress. (A few cots come with a three-position mattress base.)

- Some cots come with a teething rail. Once your baby is pulling herself up, she may make a habit of soothing her gums by gnawing on the side of the cot. A teething rail will protect the cot from damage and would also be kinder on your baby's mouth.

- It is possible to buy a cot-bed. These are slightly more expensive as they can convert to a short bed if the sides are removed. In some cases, one of the end panels can be replaced with a smaller 'foot' that is purchased as part of the package. Depending on the size of your child, once converted the bed should last until the child is seven. A cot-bed can be a cost-effective purchase if you do not think you will need the cot for another baby before the first child has grown out of the bed.

- Some cots have a 'roll-under' drop-side. These are designed to be positioned next to your own bed so that you can easily reach your baby at night. However, you will need to check that the cot mattress is level with that of your bed if this is an option that suits you.

- You may wish to choose a cot that comes on castors to make it easily movable around the nursery. Make sure that at least two of the castors can be locked to ensure safety once your baby turns into a bouncy toddler.

- If space is an issue, it is possible to buy a smaller cot or a corner-position cot. The downside of a corner cot is that it may not be so easy to get hold of the bed-linen.

• Some cots are part of a complete range of nursery furniture and this may be something you wish to consider.

Some of the cheaper cots come in an unfinished pine so that you can either paint or varnish the cot to suit your own décor. Make sure that you allow at least eight weeks for any paint or varnish to dry before you place your baby in such a cot. This will allow the new finish to dry and harden completely and, more importantly, it will allow the fumes to disperse.

• You may also wish to buy a travel cot. Check that it really is easy to transport – can it be folded away easily? Is it lightweight to carry? Does it require special-size linen? Is it small enough to be stored away when not in use?

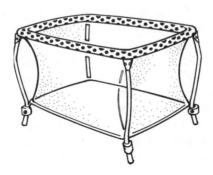

Mattresses

In most cases, the cot you have chosen will not come with a mattress and you will need to buy this separately. This is partly because you can then chose the type of mattress your baby will sleep on and partly because prices vary depending on the type. There are four basic types of cot mattress detailed below. The choice is yours but here are some things for you to consider:

Foam
- Cheap and comfortable.
- As your baby gets heavier, some of the very cheapest foam mattresses may dent into the shape of your baby's natural sleeping position.
- May only come with a wipe-clean PVC cover.
- More expensive mattresses may have a removable fabric cover that can be washed.
- Again, at the higher price band, some foam mattresses have a cushioned top layer.

Natural
- These usually have a coconut fibre core covered in other layers of wool and/or latex.
- Check that there is a waterproof membrane or that the cover is waterproof and removable for washing.
- They can be more expensive.
- If you have inherited a family cot that needs a new mattress,

it may not take a standard modern mattress size. It may therefore be best to have a natural mattress made to measure.

Spring interior
- These have a coiled-spring core that is encased in layers of foam, cotton, and/or natural fibre.
- Some only have a wipe-clean cover, others may have PVC one side and a more natural finish on the other.
- They come in a wide variety of prices, depending on their construction.

Hollowfill
- Ideal for families where asthma and allergies are a problem as these are non-allergenic.
- The non-toxic hollowfill does not absorb moisture.
- If allergies are a problem, make sure that the mattress cover is removable to allow frequent washing to keep dust mites at bay.

Golden rules for mattresses
Whatever your choice of mattress, always follow the following golden rules.
- Make sure the mattress fits the cot. Standard sizes are available and these should be labelled clearly on both the cot and the mattress. An ill-fitting mattress can be dangerous.
- Fit the mattress with a waterproof layer to make it more hygienic.

- A PVC cover on a mattress is practical as it can be easily wiped clean. However, it does not take away the moisture and heat from a baby.
- Place your baby 'back to sleep'. In other words, encourage your baby to sleep on her back to reduce the likelihood of cot death.
- Place your baby 'feet to foot'. Most baby's tend to wriggle and move downwards in their sleep. Make up the cot-linen so that your baby sleeps with her feet touching the end of the cot, thus preventing the baby from moving down and slipping her head under the covers.

- Position the cot away from the direct heat of a radiator and also away from a window. This will prevent your baby from getting too hot or too cold.
- Ensure that the cot is not going to be exposed to direct sunlight.
- Regularly wipe the mattress cover clean or wash the removable cover.
- Never use a second-hand mattress.
- Consider buying a new mattress for each child to use the cot.

Some parents prefer their baby to sleep in their bed during the first few weeks. Recent research and advice on cot death suggests that this is not always wise. Your baby could overheat and, if you are extremely tired, you may fall into a deep sleep and roll on to your baby. Ultimately though, the choice is yours – discuss it with your midwife and health visitor. Certainly, you should never sleep with your baby if you are a smoker, have taken medication which may make you drowsy, or have recently been drinking alcohol.

Cot-linen

Once you have decided on the décor of your nursery, you can choose your baby's cot-linen. Remember that most cots come in a standard size; so, too, will cot-linen. However, if you have chosen a larger-than-average cot, or perhaps a special corner cot, you will need to buy special linen, probably made by the manufacturer of the cot. If you are in doubt, check with the shop where you bought the cot – better still, check when you are buying it. If you decide on a cot-bed, you may also need to buy slightly longer sheets and blankets – again check at the time of purchase.

Because your baby will occasionally have a leaking nappy, perhaps may be very dribbly at times, or may even be prone to posseting, it's a good idea to have at least three, probably four of each of the basic items.

- Cot sheets
- Fitted bottom sheets
- Blankets

It is dangerous for a young baby or toddler to sleep with a pillow. In fact, your child will almost certainly not need a pillow until they move into a 'grown-up' bed.

Types of linen
It is probably best to get cotton sheets. These are kinder on the skin and wash very easily. If you are careful about how you hang them to dry, you can even get away with the minimum of ironing. The most common types are flannelette and terry.

- Flannelette, which are 100 per cent cotton and feel soft and warm to the touch. They wash well and are hard wearing.

- Terry, which have a 'knitted' appearance and make wonderful fitted bottom sheets as they stretch to fit the mattress. Because of the stretch effect they will not be pure cotton – but try to make sure that there is at least 80 per cent cotton in the mix.

Blankets come in a huge variety – you can buy synthetic or pure wool or cotton. You can also buy them patterned, appliquéd or plain. There are so many wonderful ones to choose from. It's a good idea to have at least two cellular ('holely') blankets made from cotton. These tend to be used in maternity hospitals as they allow air to circulate and therefore make it easier to help regulate the temperature. You may also wish to have polyester fleece blankets.

Other nursery items

When you visit a nursery store or department, you will see an array of beautiful 'nurseries' set up on display. These can give you a great idea of how your completed nursery will look at home and will show cots decorated with all sorts of extras. The items listed above are, really, the only things that you actually need for your baby. However, you may be tempted to consider some of the following items.

Cot bumper

This goes around the head end of the cot and usually co-ordinates with other linen and décor. It is essential that a cot bumper is tied securely in place – and that you check on this regularly. On no account leave a cot bumper in a cot with a baby that can sit up.

Cot drapes
These are usually fitted to a special rod that attaches to the cot although, if drapes are important to you, check that they can be fitted when you buy your cot. Drapes look pretty but can be dust-collectors in the folds of fabric so you will need to check for this regularly.

Cot duvet
These should *never* be used for a baby under 12 months.

Sleeping bag
These are popular in Europe and, once your baby is in sleepwear, you pop her into a zip up 'bag' that fits over her shoulders so that her arms are free. In order to stop your baby overheating, there should be no sleeves or hood. There should be plenty of room in the 'bag' to allow your child to move her feet and legs – so you will need to make sure that the bag is the correct size. This shouldn't be a problem because they come in sizes ranging from newborn to at least three years. Sleeping bags can be handy if your baby tends to wriggle free from the bed-linen and then wakes in the night from cold. Also, if you have used a sleeping bag from a young age, it can prevent an

older baby from climbing out of the cot. Check that the sleeping bag has the right tog value for the time of year: 0.5-1 tog for summer and 2.2-2.5 togs for winter.

Sheepskin

Once recommended as a cosy bottom layer for your baby to sleep on, these are now frowned upon by midwives and health visitors.

A room or nursery thermometer is both cheap and essential. If you buy one from a nursery store, it will not only give you a temperature reading but it will also have a simple chart and colour code reading that will tell you at a glance if your baby's room is too cold, too hot or just the right temperature. You can then adjust the heating and/or bed-linen accordingly.

Getting the temperature right

When you use this chart, remember that you need to take your baby's sleepwear into account as well. In the winter, a terry sleepsuit over a cotton bodysuit will probably be sufficient. A cotton sleepsuit will be fine in summer – if it is a very hot summer, you may want to let your baby sleep in only a bodysuit or perhaps just her nappy.

10–14°C	One top sheet plus four layers of blankets
14–18°C	One top sheet plus three layers of blankets
18°C	One top sheet plus two layers of blankets
18–26°C	One top sheet plus one layer of blanket
27°C	One top sheet only

The ideal temperature for a baby's room is under 20°C – somewhere between 16°C and 20°C should be OK. If you think your baby is cold, do not give them a hot water bottle or an electric blanket. Check the room thermometer and then adjust the bed-linen accordingly. Use the chart above as guidance. Your midwife or health visitor will also give you advice. Remember that babies can have cold hands and feet but may still be the right temperature. It is usually dangerous to let your baby sleep in a hat – only do this if you have been instructed to by your midwife.

Remember that these are a guide only. Always discuss the temperature of your baby and her nursery with your midwife and health visitor. The Foundation for the Study of Infant Death (FSID) offers advice on sleep safety. Call 020 7233 2090 or click on to www.sids.org.uk/fsid.

Baby monitors

You can't always make frequent checks on your baby when she is sleeping. If you live in a flat or small house, it may be that you can quite easily hear your baby crying or babbling once she has woken up. But, if you are in the garden or another part of the house where you are some distance from your child, you may find that a baby monitor is an essential item. Each baby monitor comes with two units: one for the nursery room and the other to be kept where the adult is. There are various types of monitor available.

Most monitors work off radio waves which means that you can often get interference from other monitors. This is usually in the form of hearing another baby crying – but you may also pick up your neighbour's television or even a conversation in another home. This can be irritating but can perhaps be restricted if you switch channels or use the monitor for visual monitoring only. But remember, if you can hear them, they may also be able to hear you. So be careful about conversations about the neighbours!

- Check that the monitor has at least two channels. If you live in a built up area, it is possible that your monitor will pick up another in use in a nearby home. If this is the case, switching channels may help.
- Some monitors are portable, which allows you to clip the adult unit to your clothing so that you can work in the garden or in a more mobile fashion. Obviously these work with batteries so always check that the batteries are still charged.
- Rechargeable units are also available; again, check that it is charged before use.

Position the nursery unit in a safe place away from the cot. You don't want your baby to pull on the flex and bring the unit down on herself.

- Check that the adult monitor has a volume control and adjust this as necessary. Some units come with a light facility which allows you to see how hard your baby is crying. This can be handy if you have friends round and want to keep a check on your baby but without everyone else being conscious of it.
- Some nursery monitors come with a built in nightlight on the nursery unit.
- It is possible to buy a monitor with a room thermometer included in the functions.
- Movement monitors are also available. These comprise a sensor mat that is placed on the mattress under your baby's bed-linen. If your baby fails to move after 20 seconds, an alarm sounds. Be cautious though – such a monitor could make you more stressed than necessary.
- Some monitors offer sound and vision in the form of a television unit that relays what the camera unit in the nursery room can see. Other vision monitors give you the opportunity of using radio waves to relay pictures to your ordinary television. Either is a very expensive way of checking on your baby, but could come in useful if you have mobility problems that prevent you from making quick checks on your baby yourself.

- Two-way monitors allow you to talk with your partner from either monitor. This could be useful if you are nursing a sick baby or perhaps if you have had a caesarean and need assistance with your partner or carer who may be in another part of the home.

A baby monitor is not a substitute for proper infant supervision. You cannot leave your child alone at home and 'keep an ear out' for them. Remember, too, that a baby monitor alone cannot prevent cot death (also known as Sudden Infant Death Syndrome or SIDS). Your health visitor or doctor will go through the precautions that are known to help in the prevention of Sudden Infant Death.

Chapter 7
Bathtime and Nappy Changing

Some newborn babies find bathtime relaxing from the start – others scream their heads off. Whichever kind of baby you have, your baby will soon start to enjoy kicking and splashing in the water. In fact, it won't be long before your baby screams when he is taken out of it.

Baby baths

When your baby is newborn, you could get away with washing him in a clean washing-up bowl or a large wash-basin (although be careful of your baby's delicate head and skin on hot, hard taps). But there are lots of items around that will make bathtime safe and less stressful for you and your newborn.

Never leave a baby unattended in the bath – even if he is secured into a bath seat or rest.

• There are lots of solid plastic baby baths around that come in a range of colours, often with co-ordinating extras such as potties and toddler steps. You may find it easier to put the baby bath into the main bath to wash your baby, simply because it will make it easier to empty afterwards. Alternatively, you can buy stands for the bath to sit on – and these certainly make life more comfortable for you.

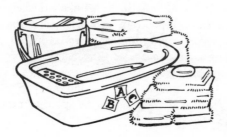

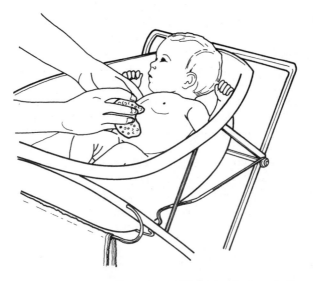

● Some solid baths are round (almost like a bucket) and allow the baby to sit on his bottom facing the person bathing him. This can make a newborn baby feel more secure in his surroundings and, because of the smaller surface area, the water in the bath will stay warmer for longer. However, if your baby grows quickly, he will soon outgrow this type of bath because it won't allow him the space he needs to kick and splash as he gets bigger.

- You can also buy a small inflatable bath – a bit like a dinghy. You'll need some puff to inflate it but it is very soft and comfortable for a baby to lie in. No one's got time to blow up the bath everyday, so you'd have to have somewhere to keep the bath when it is not in use. However, this type of bath would be very handy if you are likely to travel a lot with your baby or perhaps to keep at a grandparent's house.

- Whether you bath your baby in their own bath or the family bath, you may find it easier to use a bath support for your baby. These are made of non-slip rubber and sit in the bath, allowing you to lay your baby on top. Instantly, you have both hands free to wash your baby.

- Once your baby is able to sit unaided, you could use a special baby bath seat. This has suction pads on the bottom to prevent it moving and the baby literally sits inside this so that

a supportive ring goes around him, preventing him from falling over. Again, you have your hands free to concentrate on bathing.

- Once your baby is big enough to go in the family bath, a bath mat is probably essential. These have suction pads to make them secure on the floor of the bath. An alternative to a bath mat is to use a collection of little bath mats (usually each the size of a beer mat). These come in a number of designs and can co-ordinate with your bathroom or nursery décor.

- A bath thermometer takes the worry out of guessing. You can either get one which floats in the bath or one which sticks to the side (although you will need to make sure it is sufficiently immersed in the water to make a reading).

Bath toys

There is a huge selection of bath toys available to keep babies amused while they soak away the grime of the day.

- Make sure that all toys conform to BS standards and are suitable for babies and toddlers under 18 months (i.e. they have no small parts that could work loose and become a choking hazard).

- You'll need somewhere to keep your baby's toys when they are not in use and you want to have a long, grown-up soak. Find something to keep them in – perhaps a waterproof box or a net that fits to the splashback tiles with suction pads.

Toiletries

Your midwife and health visitor will show you how to bath your baby safely and hygienically. Although the first few times are nerveracking, even for the calmest of mothers, bathtime soon becomes fun for both you and your baby. You'll need some basic toiletries for your baby's washing and changing routine.

Baby bath
Use this instead of soap – it makes soft bubbles in the bath and gently washes away any grime.

Baby soap
This is specially formulated to be mild enough for your baby's skin.

Baby shampoo
If your baby doesn't have much hair, you could probably get away with using baby bath to wash away gently any cradle cap. But, once the hair grows thicker, you will probably prefer to use a gentle baby shampoo.

Baby talc
Not essential, but you may like to use it in your baby's 'creases' to make sure that all the moisture has been safely absorbed.

Baby lotion
Use this if your baby's skin seems slightly dry or with cotton-wool to clean your baby's bottom during nappy changes.

Newborn babies have very sensitive skin and harshly perfumed toiletries can do more harm than good. Always use products specifically designed for babies and, preferably, hypoallergenic ones. If your baby's skin seems particularly dry, discuss this with your midwife or health visitor. It may be that you should avoid products with lanolin or maybe that you need to put an emollient into your baby's bath.

Baby oil

Again, this is not essential but it can be used for cleaning your baby's bottom.

> If you use an oil in the bath – either for you or your baby – make sure that you clean the bath adequately afterwards. An oily bath will be slippery – for anyone using it.

Baby moisturiser

If you are using a mild enough product to wash your baby, you shouldn't really need this. However, during winter months, you may wish to rub a little of this into your baby's skin to protect it.

Cotton-wool

Ideal for cleaning your baby's creases, you should try to get a pure cotton version rather than a cotton mix as it will be kinder to your baby's delicate skin. Cotton-wool can come in a long strip so that you tear of what you need, or it can come already rolled into balls. The choice is yours.

Cotton buds

These are little batons or sticks with pure cushioned cotton on either end. Again these are handy for cleaning your baby's creases, especially when your baby is tiny. On no account should cotton buds be placed inside your baby's or toddler's ears.

Baby wipes

These come in a refillable tub and are sheets already coated in baby lotion. You simply pull one out of the tub, wipe your baby clean and throw them away. Extremely handy, you can also get a travel-size container that can be kept in your nappy changing bag for when you are out and about. Baby wipes are easy to use and very convenient. However, they do exactly the same job as cotton-wool and baby lotion – only more expensively.

> A wash mitt or baby sponge or flannel will help to make bathtime easier.

Baby brush and comb

Both of these will be just the right size and softness for your baby's downy hair.

Baby scissors or clippers

Baby scissors have short, round-ended blades which are delicate and small enough to cut your baby's nails. Alternatively, you may find it easier to cut the nails on your wriggling baby with a special, small pair of clippers.

Getting dry

If you can prise your baby out of the bath, you'll need to wrap him to keep him warm as he dries.

- You will need at least two baby towels: one that's dry to use and the other that's drying.
- You could use an ordinary family bath towel if you prefer.
- Baby bath towels come in finer towelling that is very soft for your baby's skin.
- You can buy towels to co-ordinate with your baby's nursery.
- Some baby towels have a hood sewn into one corner of the towel allowing you to place this over your baby's head and then envelope him snugly with the rest of the towel.

Remember that using a fabric conditioner can make your towels smell nice and feel softer, but it can also make the towels less absorbent.

Dental hygiene

Some babies start teething from an early age, others may wait for months. Whatever age your baby is, you should follow sensible dietary precautions to protect your baby's teeth and gums right from the start.

- Never add sugar to food, drinks or medicines.
- If you need to use any medications, always ask your pharmacist if a sugar-free and colour-free formula is available.
- Offer water or milk to drink rather than squashes or fruit juice.
- Never allow your baby to 'cruise' for hours over a bottle. If the feed is not taken in a sensible sitting, take the bottle away.
- Never use a dummy that has a small feeding bottle attached. Any juice offered in such a bottle will merely sit on your baby's gums, rotting the teeth inside them or, if your baby already has teeth, the drink will sit behind the teeth and rot them in situ.
- Start to clean your baby's teeth as soon as they appear – even if there is only one of them.

Cleaning baby teeth

It is never too early to start cleaning your baby's teeth, but milk teeth and sore gums that are busy producing more teeth need special, gentle care. Remember:

- Use a special baby toothbrush. This will have a small head and very soft bristles.

- Some baby toothbrushes have short, stubby handles that are perfectly designed for toddlers' hands to use. This is a great idea once your baby is ready to start learning how to clean his own teeth. However, you can buy baby toothbrushes with small, soft heads but with a longer handle more suitable for you to hold.

> While toddlers should be encouraged to hold a toothbrush and learn to brush their own teeth, this is no substitute for supervised brushing. Gently brush your baby's or toddler's teeth yourself, making sure that you clean behind as well as in front of top and bottom teeth. Don't neglect the teeth at the back either. And just like yours, a baby's teeth should be cleaned after breakfast and before bed.

- A finger toothbrush could be the easiest way to brush a very young baby's teeth. This is made of very soft silicon and slips on to your finger, rather like the finger on a rubber glove, offering a great way to get access into a tiny mouth.

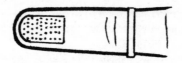

- Use a special baby toothpaste. This will be gentle in taste, should be sugar-free (check the packaging) and low in fluoride.
- Replace your baby's toothbrush regularly. This will ensure that the bristles are still up to the job of cleaning and also ensure good hygiene. An old toothbrush can allow germs to fester.
- Use a separate toothbrush for each baby or toddler.

> Check with your dentist to find out the earliest date that he or she will want to see your baby for a check-up. Good dental hygiene is a habit – and the earlier that habit begins the better.

Nappies

Nappies are a great generation test. Your granny probably swears by traditional terry nappies and your mother was perhaps of one of the first generations to get the chance to use disposal ones. So what are you going to use for your baby? Here are the choices you face.

- Disposables are convenient and so sophisticated these days that they are unlikely to leak.
- Disposables are expensive and take up a lot of smelly space in the bin.
- You can buy special nappy bins that wrap the nappy in scented plastic as you pop it in.

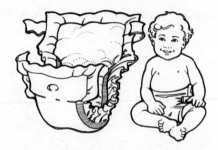

- It is thought that disposable nappies will take at least 125 years to break down in a landfill refuse site. Multiply the number of nappies you use with the number of babies in the world who are using disposables and that's a lot of rubbish for future generations to cope with.
- Some nursery stores and chemists will deliver nappies in bulk to your home.
- Disposables can be very convenient when you are travelling and away from home.
- Disposables are easy and anyone can quickly learn how to use them.
- Some mothers who use disposables say that their babies never have nappy rash.
- Because disposables are so absorbent, it can be tempting to leave your baby in them for longer than is really suitable.
- You can buy special night-time nappies for when your baby is sleeping through the night and needs more protection.

- Nowadays there is a huge choice in terry nappies – from pre-shaped nappies to all-in-ones.
- Some of the all-in-ones are very quick and easy to use and anyone can learn to use them quickly.
- Terries can be an expensive outlay at the beginning but are reused over and over again for siblings.
- Some of the newer terries come in sizes and have to be replaced as your baby grows – consider the expense of this.
- If you have more than one baby, the terries are likely to become very cost-effective.
- Whilst terries don't contribute to household waste, you will be using your washing-machine more often. This will reduce

the life of your washing-machine and increase your use of electricity.

- You will need to work out how and where you will dry the nappies once they are washed. This could be a problem if you live in a flat or during winter if you don't have a tumble-dryer or an airing cupboard.

Weigh up the pros and cons of the huge variety of nappies that faces you. In the end, you will select the type of nappy that best suits you, your lifestyle and your baby. Some mothers combine the use of disposables and terries to get the best of both worlds.

- You can buy one-way liners for terry nappies that help to keep your baby's bottom protected from moisture.
- If you clean your baby properly and change terries at regular intervals there is no reason why your baby should be more susceptible to nappy rash than a baby in disposables.
- If you have to have to change your baby while you are out, a soiled terry nappy will have to be transported home. But you can buy scented nappy sacks for this.
- Terries are a nightmare on a foreign holiday and hassle on a UK one.
- A 'nappy service' is available in some areas. They will deliver a clean supply of nappies to your door on a weekly basis and take away the soiled ones. Although this is more expensive

than buying your own, it can work out at the same price as disposables. You also won't have the washing-machine costs or the hassle. Ask your midwife or at the hospital maternity unit if there is a service like this in your area.

- Once your baby is sleeping through the night, you may have to use two terries to last them through. Or you can buy supplementary pads to absorb the extra urine.
- Some devotees of terry nappies also claim that their babies potty-trained earlier than babies in disposable nappies. This could be because a wet terry is not as comfortable as a disposable that barely feels damp.

Changing equipment

You will probably go through about six nappy changes a day –
more perhaps if your baby is teething or has an upset tummy.
So, working out where you are going to change your baby as
quickly, comfortably and conveniently as possible is a priority.
Your granny may have changed your mum's nappy on her lap
but you don't have to be quite so gymnastic these days.

- You can change a baby on a towel or blanket on either a
  draught-free floor or a bed. This is fine until your baby wees
  without the nappy being under him.
- A PVC-coated changing mat is not expensive and is a
  comfortable and waterproof way to cope with a nappy change.
- You can buy changing tables or units. These have shelves and
  drawers beneath them where you can store clean nappies and
  your baby's other changing needs. These are convenient but
  can be expensive. You may also find that your baby outgrows
  the changing unit well before outgrowing nappies.

- You can buy changing units and tables that fit into corners, that fold up flat against the wall when they are not in use or that fit securely across the top of your baby's cot.

Never leave your baby unattended on a changing mat. Even a newborn baby could fall off. As soon as your baby can roll over, you will need eyes in the back of your head when you are changing him. If you have a particularly wriggly baby, it may be safer to change nappies on a draught-free floor.

- The good thing about changing units is that they stop you from having to bend over frequently. This can be particularly useful when you are changing a newborn and perhaps have a sore back after birth. If you suffer from back problems, a changing unit may not be simply a luxury item but a necessity.
- There is no reason why you can't use a high table with a changing mat placed in the centre of it to create your own changing unit. If the table is big enough, there should be plenty of space for you to fit all your changing essentials around the changing mat, too.
- Some changing units allow the top to interchange as a changing table or baby bath.
- Some of the more expensive units match other nursery furniture and can be quite simply adapted for use as bedroom furniture when no longer required as a changing unit. So the initial financial outlay may become more cost-effective.

Changing bags

Wherever you take your baby, you will need to take a changing bag, too. You'll be carrying a lot of essential items with you when you travel, so don't be tempted to buy the first bag you see. It's not just about what the bag looks like that counts – it's what you can do with the bag that matters just as much.

- Work out how much you can put into the bag. Is there space for spare nappies as well as perhaps a change of clothing? Or would you prefer to travel with a smaller bag that has only the bare essentials in?

- Some changing bags come with their own secure bottle carrier – which can be handy if you want to avoid buying a separate carrier or having a leaking bottle all over the contents of the bag.

- Does the bag come complete with a fold-up changing mat?

- Is the bag sufficiently well made to last the length of time that you will be carrying it around?

- Can the bag be used as a back pack? You may find this useful if you are out and about a lot.

- Can the bag be machine-washed or at least wiped clean?

- Are there separate compartments in the bag to help keep everything neat and tidy?

- Some bags come with a separate smaller bag for holding dummies or other smaller items. These bags can be handy for all sorts of small things that you want to get quick access to. The bag can also be attached to the larger bag.

Potties

You will change a lot of nappies in your baby's life, but there will come a time when he is ready to try sitting on a potty. You will no doubt be given a lot of advice from other mothers about how and when they trained their own babies to use a potty – listen to all of it and then, to a large extent, ignore it, especially if it doesn't suit you or your baby. Some very bright babies manage to potty train as early as 17 months – but other baby's aren't interested until they are at least two-and-a-half.

You may know instinctively when your baby is due to come out of nappies: your baby may start to realise that 'dirty' nappies are uncomfortable and comment as soon as their nappy is in this state. (If you are lucky enough to have a baby with this sensitivity, it might take much longer for your baby to realise that wet nappies are also uncomfortable.) Alternatively, you may wish to wait until summer months mean that your baby can wander around without a nappy and 'bottom' clothing, thus encouraging him to notice when he wees. If you have another baby on the way though, you may want to encourage potty training so that it is out of the way before the next baby arrives and so that you aren't changing two lots of nappies.

When you think that you and your baby are ready to try, introduce the potty at a nappy changing time when you and your baby are not stressed and in a hurry. Comment and congratulate if there is a 'success'. (Do this if your baby wees or poos when you are changing a nappy as well as it encourages them to know that something is happening and that they are making it happen.) If you think your baby is beginning to get the hang of it, try to do this every time you do a nappy change. If your baby gets agitated or is clearly uninterested, abandon potty training and try again a few weeks or months later.

It is said that successful potty training, done at the time that is right for your child, can be sorted in the space of two weeks. But even if they are dry and clean during the day, expect the occasional accident; it is the rare baby that manages to be dry at night straight away.

Your health visitor will give you tips and advice about potty training but when you are ready to try potty training, you will need to have the following things ready.

● A potty. These come in a variety of styles from the most basic to a state-of-the-art toilet system. Some potties come with lids that flip up to emulate the loo that the rest of the family sits on. Some have handles or high sides that the toddler can grip for security. Others sit securely on top of a box to make the potty higher – and the box can be used as a step-stool for when your toddler needs to reach the family toilet or the bathroom basin.

Ideally a potty should be higher at the back and have a reasonably broad and sturdy bottom to make it feel comfortable and secure for your baby. It should also have a

higher 'lip' in the middle at the front of the potty to catch any splashes, especially if your baby is a boy.

> Always clean your baby's potty thoroughly after use to keep it hygienic, especially as your baby's hands and fingers are likely to be all over it.

- A portable potty. These fold up and fit into your nappy changing bag for when you are out and about. Some come with disposable bags that need to be changed each time your baby succeeds. If you have a toddler that goes little and often, you may find that this is expensive.
- A trainer seat. These fit over the ordinary loo seat to make it small and secure for your toddler to sit on and feel like a grown-up. They can come as part of a complete toilet training system or be bought separately. Some seats attach to the hinges of the family seat so that they can simply be

flipped up when your toddler isn't using it. Other seats are soft and warm to the touch, making the toilet experience more comfortable for your toddler.

- A portable toilet seat. This folds up and pops into a bag when not in use, ideal for when you are out and about or on holiday.
- A musical potty. Not an essential item but a novelty one as it plays a tune when something hits the bottom. Expensive, but if you think it will make your toddler learn the art of using a potty, you may want to try it.

Chapter 8
Feeding

Discuss with your midwife the various options you have for feeding your baby. Research has proved that breastfeeding is best for your baby, certainly in the first few days and preferably weeks and months of your baby's life. Not only is breastfeeding more convenient for both you and your baby, it also provides essential nutrients and passes on your own immunities to help protect your baby. But, for most new mothers, breastfeeding takes practice before both parties are comfortable with it. Again, your midwife will be able to give you guidance to make sure that your baby is latching on properly to make sure that the feeding is successful. If you are a member of the National Childbirth Trust (NCT), you will also be put in touch with a breastfeeding counsellor who will be able to help you with any problems that you may have. Here are some ideas of things that will help you make the best of breastfeeding your baby.

- You will need some breastpads to slip into your bra for when you are breastfeeding. These will absorb any 'leaks' from your breasts in between feeds.
- You can buy both disposable or washable breastpads. Both should be comfortable and it is really personal preference

which you choose. You will want to make sure that any washable ones have a high cotton content and can be tumble-dried for speed. Some washable pads come complete with a washing-bag which prevents them from getting lost in the rest of the washing.

- You may be wise to buy some nipple cream to prevent sore, cracked nipples. There is a large choice available; recent research has advised that you should avoid any ointments that contain peanut oil as this has been linked with allergies in children.

- If you have a problem with inverted nipples, it is possible to buy a shield called a Nipplette, which you wear inside your bra for a while. This is a comfortable and safe way to correct your nipples, ready for breastfeeding. If you have a problem with inverted nipples, discuss it with your midwife during your pregnancy as you need to correct this before birth.

- Breast shells or nipple protectors can also help if you have sore breasts when you start breastfeeding. These are made of silicone and protect sore and cracked nipples during breastfeeding.

- A breast pump may sound a bit intimidating but will allow a breastfeeding mother a break from her baby to go out. Breast pumps come as either manual or battery operated but all work in the same basic way: a silicon dome or cushion fits over your breast and the pump simulates your baby's suckling movements. The breast milk is then collected directly into a bottle which is attached to the pump. Make sure that the breast pump can be kept sterile if you need to take it about with you.

A breast pump can be an essential piece of equipment if you are planning to return to work. By expressing milk, or by collecting excess milk at a time when your baby doesn't need it, you can continue to breastfeed your baby when you return to work. Some babies may be reluctant to take milk from a bottle when they are first confronted with one but they will soon sense your 'smell' in the milk and that, combined with their hunger, will soon get them suckling from a bottle.

- Some breast pumps are for use with disposable bottle bags. These can be a useful way of safely freezing the milk for later use. When the milk is defrosted, the bottle bag simply fits into a holder, has a teat attached and is ready for your baby.

Formula milk

If you decide to bottle-feed, or perhaps offer your baby a combination of breast and bottle-feeds, your midwife or health visitor will advise you on the formula milks that are available. You may find that once your baby has a taste for one brand, she will not want to swap it for another without problems.

Formula milk powder must only be mixed with recently boiled water. Only boil the water once before you use it to make up the formula.

- Most formula milk comes in powder form and should be mixed with recently boiled water using sterilised equipment.
- If you have a very hungry baby, your health visitor may advise you to use a formula milk that has thicker curds that satisfy your baby more. Only use these under your health visitor's instruction.
- Some of the formula milks are also available ready mixed. This is a more expensive way of buying it but it can be very useful if you are on holiday or out and about. The cartons are sterilised and ready to pour straight into a sterile bottle. All you have to do then is heat to your baby's preferred temperature.
- You may be able to buy formula milk at the baby clinic for a lower price.
- Never use any formula milk that has had the seal broken before you get it home.
- Always check that the formula milk is within the 'use by' date indicated on the packet.

Allow the prepared bottles to cool before you store them in the fridge. Putting hot bottles into the fridge will raise the temperature of everything else in the fridge and could be dangerous.

Bottles

Even if you plan to breastfeed, it is advisable to buy a few bottles to have at the ready. There is an enormous selection of bottles and teats available and it is best to decide on the one make that you prefer and then stick to this, as the bottles are usually part of a greater feeding system in which parts are interchangeable.

- If you are buying a breast pump, it may only work with one system of bottles, so bear this in mind when choosing other bottles.
- Newborn babies drink smaller quantities of milk and you may find it easier to feed them from smaller bottles. These are usually as wide as the taller bottles as they take the same caps and teats.
- Smaller bottles can be useful for giving your baby cooled, boiled water.
- In some feeding systems, the smaller bottles can also double up as food storage jars.
- Can the same larger bottles be used with a handle fitment for when your baby is ready to start holding her bottle herself?

Never leave a baby alone with a bottle – even when the baby is able to hold the bottle on her own. You should never leave a bottle in the corner of the cot – even for an older baby that occasionally wakes in the night for a thirst-quenching drink. Your baby could choke if left unattended.

- You may prefer to buy translucent coloured or patterned bottles for your baby.
- Some bottles come with a very wide neck and therefore have a chubby appearance. These can be handy for when your baby starts to hold his own bottle as they usually come with a handle attachment and also a feeding spout for when your

baby is starting to drink from a feeder cup rather than through a teat. However, you may not find it comfortable to hold a wider bottle when you are feeding a newborn baby.

- A bottle brush is an essential piece of equipment to safely clean bottles before sterilising. An ordinary washing-up brush may not fit down the neck of the bottles or may not fit around the curves of the bottle.

- You can also buy a teat brush (in fact this may come as part of a bottle brush set). This a small brush designed to fit right into the teat to clean away the milk deposits.

Teats

Teats are usually a universal size (although you will need to get teats for the wider neck system if that is what you plan to use) but come in two varieties: rubber and silicone. As with the type of bottles you use, the choice is yours but once you start using one type with your baby, you may find that they are reluctant to change or alternate between the two.

- Teats come in three 'speeds' of delivering the milk as your baby sucks. This is dictated by the size of the hole in the teat and is defined as slow, medium and fast-flow.
- Newborn babies usually prefer to use slow-flow teats.
- Adjust the flow of the teat as your baby grows and develops. If your baby is a very hungry baby or seems to be taking longer or working harder at sucking, it may mean that you need to move up to a faster flowing teat. Ask your health visitor or midwife for advice.
- You should clean the inside of used teats by gently rubbing them with salt before you sterilise them.
- Remember that teats don't last for ever and will need replacing after a while. When a teat is reaching the end of its life it may start 'collapsing' as your baby sucks or it may start to feel sticky to the touch.

Sterilisers

Just like bottles, there are many different types of sterilisers. Whatever system you use, it is essential that you sterilise your baby's bottles and teats. These are your choices.

Chemical sterilisers

These are like plastic tanks that you fill with your baby's bottles and teats (and any other feeding paraphernalia) and then fill with cold water. A sterilising tablet is then dropped into the tank and the lid put on. After the time indicated, you remove the now sterile equipment.

This is a cheap way of sterilising your baby's bottles but you must make sure that no air bubbles are trapped in the bottles and teats, thus preventing complete sterilisation. After chemical sterilisation, you will have to rinse everything with recently boiled water to rinse off the chemical. This can be awkward. Also, remember that a cold water steriliser will be very heavy once it is filled with equipment and water so you will need to have space to keep it near the kitchen sink.

Steam sterilisers

These are quick and easy to use and destroy the bacteria via the intense heat of the steam. You will need to have a spare electrical socket that is easy to access. Most units come with the plug ready fitted and some come with a pair of tongs that allow you to remove the items without contamination.

These machines usually produce sterile equipment within minutes of switching on but remember that the bottles will only remain sterile for a couple of hours after the machine is switched off. Refer to the manufacturer's instructions for full information about the machine you are considering.

These units are often very hot to the touch when they have completed their cycle. You will also need to take care when removing the lid from the machine as residual steam may be left inside and this could burn your face and hands.

> Check that the sterilising unit you choose is big enough to take a breast pump and also any spoons and small bowls that you may use for weaning your baby.

Microwave sterilisers

These work in your domestic microwave so you will need to check that the sterilising unit can fit within the confines of your microwave's oven and, if it has a turntable, that the unit can also turn properly without getting caught. You will also need to check that your microwave oven is not too powerful for the wattage that the unit can take. These units work in a similar way to a steam unit: you fill the unit with the bottles and teats and then fill a cavity with water, the steam that is created while the microwave is working kills the bacteria.

Because you will need to put water into the unit before you place it into the microwave, work out whether it is going to be practical for you to get the unit from the sink to the microwave without spillage. Microwave sterilisers need to be loaded in exactly the same order each time to ensure that sterilisation is successful. This may be fiddly at first but you should soon get used to it. You will also need to check that the bottle and feeding system that you use is suitable for microwaves.

Travel sterilisers

You will still need to sterilise when you are on holiday so you may wish to borrow or buy a travelling unit. These are smaller and more compact than home units and are available in both cold water and microwave options.

Microwave sterilisation bags

These are a boon for mothers who breastfeed and may only have a few items to sterilise. These can be stored completely flat when not in use and can take up to two bottles. Each bag can be used up to 20 times. As with all systems, you must follow the instructions properly to ensure proper sterilisation.

Dual sterilisers

It is possible to buy one unit which allows you to both cold sterilise and microwave sterilise your bottles. This could be handy if you think that you may use the unit on holiday where a microwave may not be available.

Other bottle-feeding equipment

You will soon get into a routine with your baby's feeding and there are some other non-essential items that can help to make your life easier.

Bottle warmers

You will probably make up your baby's bottles in batches and then store them in the fridge. In advance of the time of the feed, you will need to heat your baby's bottle up and your grandmother and possibly your mother did this by heating the bottle in a pan of hot water or by placing the bottle in a jar of hot water. Now, this can be done in a bottle warmer. You simply place the bottle in the warmer and it quickly heats the bottle to the temperature that you have dictated on the dial.

Some bottle warmers can also take jars of both home-made and manufactured baby food.

You can heat your baby's bottle in the microwave oven. Remember to remove the top and teat before you do so and also to shake the bottle once it is heated and the bottle is reassembled. 'Hot spots' can occur in a microwaved bottle and it is essential to avoid these as they can burn your baby's delicate mouth, throat and stomach – hence you have to shake the bottle. Refer to the manufacturer's instructions about the safe heating of baby bottles and also discuss this with your midwife or health visitor to ask their safety advice.

Portable bottle warmers

These come in two options. The first is more traditional and looks like a vacuum flask. You can store the water in the flask as soon as it is boiled and then, when you are ready to heat the bottle, you simply pop the bottle into the lid and wait for a few minutes while the bottle heats to the right temperature. This can be very convenient for night feeds.

The second option works in a car's cigarette lighter socket. You simply wrap a 'heating blanket' around the bottle and then plug the system into the socket. You will need to check that your car has a lighter system though – many don't these days.

'Night and day' warmers

These have an insulated cooler which keeps up to two bottles cooled at a safe temperature. When you need to heat the bottle, you simply place it on the separate warming section; great for night feeding.

Electronic warmers
These are small and neat and fit around the bottle (and also food jars) to heat the milk.

Bottle carriers
These provide insulation to keep bottles either warm or cold when you are out and about. Different sizes are available to either take a single bottle or two.

Muslin squares
These have so many uses you will wonder if you can ever do without them. Ideal for quickly wiping a bottle when it is removed from a bottle warmer, these can also be used as an improvised bib to catch drips and dribbles as your baby feeds. They can also be placed on your shoulder or under your baby's chin when you 'wind' your baby after a feed. Pop a muslin square in your nappy bag as well – they are essential for wiping all kinds of spills and slops.

Soothers
Some babies are comforted by sucking and they may want or even need to do this even when they are not hungry. If your own baby is like this, she may 'find' her own thumb or finger

and may be contented with sucking on this in between feeds. Other babies may be more contented if they are introduced to a soother – these are also known as dummies and pacifiers.

The world seems to be divided into two when it comes to soothers – people either couldn't care less about them or hate them with a vengeance. However you feel about them before your baby is born, you may find that when your baby cannot settle on their own, or perhaps has very sore gums, your baby contentedly sucking on a soother may save your sanity. So keep an open mind and do what is best for you and your baby.

- Always make sure that the dummy is sterile, especially when your baby is very young.
- Ensure that the soother has a teat which allows the natural development of your baby's teeth, palate and gums.
- A special chain can attach to your baby's clothes or pram to ensure that the soother cannot get lost.
- If your baby takes to a soother, make sure that you have at least two or three of the same type so that you can ensure they are clean and sterile.

A teething ring may be another item that is comforting to a teething baby. This may have a soft, chewy surface or perhaps a gel-filled ring that can ease sore gums. Some teething rings can be placed in the fridge and babies can find the coldness soothing when their gums are aching.

- Choose a soother that is the appropriate size for your baby, following the age guidelines on the packaging.
- Some soothers come in cases which allow you to carry extra clean soothers out and about with you.
- It is probably best to wean your baby off of using soothers once she starts to toddle around. This will be more hygienic. Also, the earlier you can wean a baby from using a soother, the easier it will be – you may find that you can persuade your toddler only to use a soother at night when she first settles to sleep.
- Remember that no one ever saw a 12-year-old using a soother.

Some babies find comfort in sucking a muslin square. You may be tipped off to this if your baby sucks her bed-linen. Try to avoid your baby from getting too attached to one particular muslin by constantly changing the muslin for a clean and dry one and avoid potential accidents with muslin becoming wrapped around your baby's neck by using only small pieces. Clean men's handkerchiefs are good alternatives and can also be easily swapped for a clean one.

Weaning equipment

Your health visitor and your own baby will let you know when the time is right for weaning. Usually, this is around about 16 weeks or more, but you need to get it right for both your baby's health, development and your own sanity. Introducing solids too early will not only frustrate your baby but also might not be healthy for your baby. However, if your baby was sleeping through the night and then starts to wake again for an extra feed, this could indicate that she needs something a little more substantial in her tummy than simply milk. If you leave it too late to introduce solids, you may find that your baby demands more and more milk and is grizzly and grumpy from having all that liquid slopping around his tummy. Your baby may also get lazy about trying solid food and reject it if you leave it too late. Remember, too, that, when the time is right, your baby needs the nutrients that come with solid food.

It's a good idea to get some weaning equipment and have it ready ahead of time.

- All feeding bottles come with a cap and this can make an ideal first feeding bowl for those first tastes of solid food.
- Weaning spoons are an easier and more hygienic way of feeding your baby than an adult's fingers. Some first spoons come with soft bowls that are gentle and comfortable for a baby's mouth. Don't buy a spoon that has a very deep bowl as this could offer your baby too much food for a first mouthful.
- Infant spoons and forks are designed for when your baby starts to feed herself. They often come with easy-grip handles that may be curved to encourage your toddler to hold them. They will have soft and gentle edges that cannot harm toddlers as they experiment with food and how it finds its way into their mouth.

 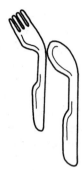

- Bowls come in a range of sizes and depths. You may find it easier to feed your baby from a bowl that has a 'holding lip' on the side. Some bowls have compartments to separate the different types of food that you may feed your baby. These are not essential when you are feeding your baby, but once your toddler is feeding herself, she can start to explore which foods she prefers if they are held separately.

- Spillproof bowls have suction pads on the bottom. Again, these are not essential when you are feeding your baby yourself but can be handy once you are letting your toddler learn to do it on her own. Remember though – they are not completely spillproof if you have a very boisterous baby.

- Stay-warm bowls have a double sided structure and a 'plug' that can be removed so that the cavity beneath the bowl can be filled with warm water. These help to keep the food warm

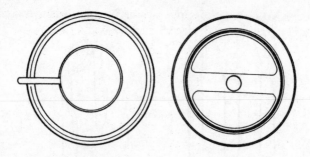

when your baby is feeding herself for the first time (which can take a while to achieve.). However, these can leave the bowl with very hot sides – so use them with caution.

- Travel bowls have lids which keep the food ready in the bowl. Remember though that you will still need to keep the bowl upright during transit. Travel bowls can be useful if you return to work and need to prepare food in advance for your baby's minder.

First beakers and training cups

If you have bought bottles that are part of a complete feeding system they will have come with a feeding spout which can replace the teat on the bottle. This will give your baby her first experience of a wider spout. Once she is used to this and can hold her own bottle, you can introduce the feeding spout on a cup that has handles. Once your baby is used to this way of drinking you are rapidly approaching the time when you can stop using bottles and start to use cups for all drinks.

- Non-spill cups are an essential both at home and when you are out and about. Whatever way the cup is tipped, the one-way valve inside the lid prevents them from spilling the contents. Some cups will also allow your child's own sipping to control the flow of the liquid so that she does not choke.

Once your baby is old enough to cope with a feeding spout rather than a teat, discourage the use of the teat. Feeding spouts are better for your baby's teeth and discourage milk and other drinks from collecting behind your baby's front teeth and forming decay.

- Flip-top cups are handy once your baby is beyond the spilling stage. The feeding spout simply flips up and down to open

119

and close. When your baby is ready, you can simply remove the top and introduce your baby to a 'cup' for the first time.

- 'Sports' bottles have a more grown up appearance and have a mouthpiece that pops up and down for drinking. Only for use by toddlers.

- Juice box holders allow you to place a small boxed container of juice into a plastic shell. You then insert the straw and the toddler sips from this. These are a less messy way of a toddler using a juice container as they cannot squeeze the sides, and also have the benefit of offering a handle to hold on to. However, branded fruit drinks and even pure fruit juices are not advisable for babies and toddlers as they are too sweet and concentrated for their teeth and gums. Follow your health visitor's advice on what is safe for your baby to drink.

Check that feeding equipment is suitable for use in the sterilising unit that you have chosen.

High-chairs

Once your baby is able to sit up safely on her own, you can introduce her to eating his meals in the safety of her own high-chair. Many high-chairs are part of a co-ordinated range of nursery equipment so you may choose one on this basis. Wooden high-chairs can look attractive and might blend in with other furniture that you have. However, plastic and metal high-chairs can be more adaptable offering various positions and foldability. Bear in mind the list overleaf when you make your selection and decide which items are a priority for your lifestyle.

Never leave your baby or toddler unattended in a high-chair and never allow your baby or toddler to be in the high-chair without being in a safety harness. Make sure that you only use a five-point safety harness that secures around your baby's waist and prevents her from slipping under the eating tray and from leaning too far forward or to the side.

- Does the eating tray slide out or lift up so that a larger baby or toddler can still be placed in and out of the chair in comfort?
- Is the eating tray easily wipeable for hygiene?
- Can the eating tray be completely removed so that the chair can then be pushed in closer to the family table when your toddler is old enough to use the table top like every one else?
- Is the seat covered in wipeable PVC?
- Is the seat padded for your baby's comfort?
- Can the padded seat be removed for when your baby is older and may prefer a more grown-up look?
- Does the high-chair fold up when not in use? (This may be essential if you have a small kitchen or dining area.)
- Does the 'high-chair' become a 'low-chair' for when your baby is older?
- Can the frame of the high-chair convert into a first swing for your baby?
- Does the chair come with its own safety harness attached or does it have 'D' rings to which another safety harness can be attached?
- If the chair has its own safety harness, can this be removed for washing?

Some two-height chairs allow the bottom half of the chair to be converted into a playtable for an older toddler to use in tandem with the chair in the low position. This can be a very cost-effective purchase.

There are alternatives to the high-chair when your baby is older.

● Clip-on seats clamp to the edge of your existing kitchen or dining table so that your toddler is eating with the rest of the family. Make sure that you check to see if the clamps can be fitted properly to your table and ensure that they are always fully secured before you place your baby into the seat. A washable seat may be more desirable.

● Booster seats can be positioned on an ordinary dining-chair or bench. Make sure that you can secure this to the seat to avoid movement once an active toddler is inside.

● Two or three-level booster seats. Although these may be more expensive they adapt (by allowing you to adjust their height) to suit your toddler as she grows.

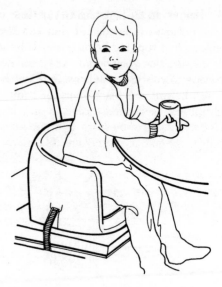

• Fold-up booster seats are ideal if you have a small kitchen and need to put things away when they are not in use. You can also use them to take out and about with you.

Always make sure that the bottom of a booster seat has non-slip rubber pads. If you choose a clip-on seat, make sure that the clamp also offers rubber or cushioned protection to protect your table top.

Other mealtime accessories

Mealtimes are fun and sociable – but they can also be messy. Remember that when the time comes, your baby will need to 'experiment' with her food to find out what she likes to eat and also to learn how it gets from the bowl and into her mouth – and hair ... up the wall ... and all over the room. The messy stage doesn't last for ever. In most cases, it only lasts for a few weeks as your baby will soon learn that she likes food. The following things can help to make your life easier.

- Bibs are an essential to protect your baby's clothes when they are eating. Some have a waterproof backing which stops the liquid from soaking through. This can make life easier but continued washing can make the PVC backing split and tear.
- Some bibs attach with Velcro fastenings. This is handy when your baby is smaller but as she grows you may find that bibs that have traditional ties are better as they adapt according to your child's growth.
- Moulded plastic bibs have a tray at the bottom that catches food as it drops down. This can mean that your baby's bottom half clothes are protected from food spills but you may find that the bib catches on the eating tray of a high-chair.
- A large PVC sheet placed underneath the high-chair as your baby eats will protect your carpet and save on having to mop any tiles or lino. Alternatively, you could use old sheets of newspaper and simply throw the lot away after every meal.

The downside of this though is that the newspaper won't be waterproof.

- Large plastic place mats are ideal for when your toddler starts to eat at the table with the rest of the family. These are wide enough to take all of your toddler's eating equipment, therefore protecting the table top. Simply wipe clean after mealtimes.

Chapter 9
Out and About with your Baby

Choosing your baby's own set of wheels and the seat in which they will safely travel in *your* wheels is one of the most important decisions you will have to make. It may well be that the car seat you choose is part of an entire travel system and that it fits into your baby's first set of pram wheels.

Whatever your ultimate decision, don't rush making up your mind, but consider the many safety and comfort factors as well as practical and style implications before you make your final choice.

Car seats
Car seats come in a variety of safety groups so you need to think about what is most suitable for you.

Group 0
These are suitable from birth and up to nine months or 10 kg/ 22 lb – whichever is the sooner. The seats are rearward facing and usually come with a carry handle to transport your baby

easily from the car to home (or even when out shopping) without having to remove your baby from the seat. These seats have an integrated five-point harness that secures your baby safely.

Group 0+
These have the same features as Group 0 but should take a baby from birth and 15 months or up to 13 kg/29 lb, whichever is the sooner.

Group 0+ and Group 1 combination seats

Suitable for use from birth to nine months or 13 kg/29 lb when used rearward facing. Once your baby is 9 kg/20 lb you can start to use the seat forward facing until your baby is 18 kg/40 lb. Combination seats also have the benefit of adjustable seat recline so that you can position your baby in a more comfortable position if he is sleeping. All of these seats will come with an integrated five-point harness.

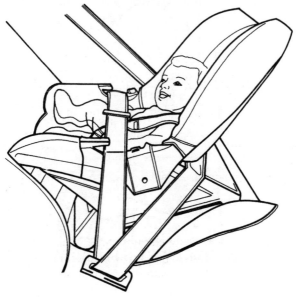

Group 1

Forward facing seats that are suitable for babies from nine months or 9 kg/20 lb. Fitted with an integrated five-point harness, some Group 1 seats may have reclining seat positions.

Group 2

Forward facing seats suitable for children from 15–25 kg/33–55 lb or from the age of four to six. These will have a fixed seat position and are lightweight, making them easy to move from one car to another or for when you don't want the seat in the car. The child is secured using the car's own three-point belt. Some of these seats come as two sections (the back and the seat) that are zipped together. As your child gets older, the seat can be used on its own as a booster seat.

Group 3

Forward facing booster seats for children from four to about 11 years of age or 15–36 kg/33–80 lb. These should be used in conjunction with the car's own three-point seat belt that will be secured into place so that it doesn't cut across your child's thighs and with the seat belt held correctly over the shoulder.

Choosing your car seat

Once you have decided on the type of system that you want to buy, bear in mind the following pointers.

- Does the safety harness do up in one simple movement? Can you also adjust it with a single adjuster strap? (Both of things can make your life simpler when you are wrestling a baby in and out of a car.)
- Are any reclining positions simple to use?

- If the seat is for a newborn, does it come complete with a headhugger to provide comfort and security for a tiny baby? If not, can you buy one separately?
- Are the covers easily removed for washing?
- If the covers wear out, will you be able to buy replacements?
- Are there extra pads that can be fitted on the chest straps and perhaps at the back of the buckle?
- If the seat uses the car's own seat belts, can it be used on both the left and right sides of the car?
- If the car's own seat belts are to be used, are the 'lock-off guides' used to secure the seat easy to use? Do they also reduce the movement of the seat once the child is secure?
- If you are choosing a Group 0 or Group 0+ seat, is it compatible with a pushchair travel system? (You may find this more useful if you need to be out and about a lot with older siblings and will be in and out of the car frequently.)

NEVER FIT A CAR SEAT IN A POSITION WHERE AIRBAGS ARE FITTED. This could kill your baby if an impact makes the bag activate. It is possible to have airbags de-activated quite simply in your car. Have this done properly by a garage – preferably by a mechanic at a garage connected to your car's manufacturer.

The car seat safety checklist

- **Never buy second-hand:** The seat may have been in an accident rendering it unsafe. It may also be old and may no longer meet current safety standards. The car seat could also have been modified in an unsafe way by a previous owner. Important components of the car seat may also be worn and subsequently be unsafe through age.

- **Always fit the seat in accordance with the manufacturer's instructions:** If the seat doesn't come with written instructions, don't buy it. Read the instructions carefully and ALWAYS fit the seat as directed – never save time and cheat as you could kill your child by doing so.

- **Never allow any of the harness or seat belt to twist:** This can reduce the effectiveness and thereby pose a risk in an accident.

- **Ask the shop if you can try out the shop's sample in your own car:** This will ensure that it fits both the seat belts and the seats themselves. The shop assistant will also be able to show you how the seat should be safely fitted in your car.

- **If you have a car accident you should probably change your child's car seat:** The seat will have absorbed the impact of the accident and the stress on the car seat could have damaged some of the components. In a subsequent accident, even a minor one, the car seat may no longer be able to live up to its job and therefore be dangerous. Check your car insurance policy as you may well find that the insurance company will replace a child seat after an accident because of this.

Car seat accessories

These can make your life neater and maybe even help you to have a stress-free journey.

Headhugger

Many Group 0/0+ seats come complete with one of these but you can buy them separately. They provide extra head support for newborn babies.

Toys

These are usually very soft fabric mobiles that attach to the handle of a Group 0/0+ car seat. But make sure the toys don't simply bump into your baby's face as you travel along.

Neck supports

For older toddlers and children, these fit snugly and softly around your child's neck and provide support should the child's head flop through travel-induced sleep.

Play Tray

Clips on to the front of a car seat to provide a flat surface for playing on. Some come complete with built-in toys.

Sunshade

Using suction pads, this can be positioned on any rear car window to provide protection from the sun.

Car tidy

These usually clip on to the back of a car seat and have a series of pockets or compartments for you to stash stray toys in.

Shoulder pads

These clip on to seat belts and provide extra comfort for older children, preventing the seat belt from cutting into their shoulders.

Prams and pushchairs

A pram or a pushchair is a major expenditure – and one that you want to be more than happy with, as it will last you a long time. Don't be rushed into buying something simply because it looks nice or someone else has told you that it has been great for them. Work out from the following list what is important to you and your lifestyle and it will help you to make the right decision.

- Will you be relying on public transport? If so, you will need a pram or pushchair that can fold up quickly and easily. Remember, too, that you may have shopping with you – can the folded up pram cope with this?

- If you will be travelling in a car, check the size of the boot to work out if the pram or pushchair will fold down small enough to fit into it.

- Once your baby's mode of transport is folded down, can you lift it easily, bearing in mind you will almost certainly be holding your baby in one arm?

- Where will you have to store the pram or pushchair? If it is going to have to live in your hallway, can it be folded up small enough to be kept at one side of the hall?

- If you have a side or garden entrance to your home, can you store the pram in a shed or perhaps have a special 'pram porch' made?

- Are you or is your partner shorter or taller than average height? This may limit your choice of pram. However, some prams and pushchairs come with adjustable handles – try some out in the shop.

- Will you be walking long distances with your newborn baby? If so, you should look for a pram that has a proper mattress to support your baby's back properly.

- Can you anticipate the type of terrain that you will be pushing along? If you are likely to spend a lot of time in shops or urban areas, you may prefer to have swivel wheels. If you are travelling along rougher ground, fixed wheels will be easier. Some prams and pushchairs give you the option of swivel or locked positions.

- If you are likely to spend a lot of time in countryside or beaches, or if you are likely to go jogging with your baby, consider an all-terrain pushchair which will have three instead of four wheels that will be much larger than average. Bear in mind that the pushchair is likely to have pneumatic tyres – and that these can puncture. You may need to carry a bicycle repair kit around with you.

- Do you want your baby or toddler to face you or the direction that they are being pushed? Some prams and pushchairs give you the option of swapping about.
- Think about the handles on prams and pushchairs. Some are soft and padded, others are smooth and hard.
- Some pushchairs offer reclining seat positions – is this likely to be important to you and your baby?
- Check out the suspension on various prams and pushchairs and see if you have a preference. Some offer a hard ride, others soft, some even give you adjustable suspension.
- Will you have a toddler and a newborn? In which case, should you buy a double pushchair that allows one of the children to lie flat and the other upright? If so, will it be easier for you to cope with a vehicle in which one child travels in front of the other (easier to get through shop doorways) or perhaps one where the children travel side by side (which may be able to umbrella-fold when not in use).
- An older toddler may be able to travel on a buggy board attached to the back of your pushchair or buggy. Check to see if one of these can be fitted to a pushchair at a later date.
- Do you have older children that you have to take to and collect from school? If you will need to have lots of short car journeys and then have to stand around in the playground, you may want to invest in a travel system so that your baby can be transported to and from the car, straight into the system's wheels with little disturbance.

Just like car seats, prams and pushchairs come in a variety of types. There are eight basic types from which to choose.

Hard-bodied prams

These are the state-of-the-art traditional prams that come with a long, wide, hard body and large wheels. They are a doddle to push because they have proper suspension and just glide along. They are also extremely comfortable and secure for your baby as well. But – big but – they are very large and very expensive and most homes no longer have the space to store them. The other major downside is that they don't come apart to fit into the car either.

> It may be possible to get an excellent second-hand pram or pushchair at a very reasonable price. However, only consider buying either from a friend whom you really trust to be telling you the truth about the pram's history, or from a reputable nursery shop that specialises in part-exchange and second-hand prams.

Complete travel systems

These are the most expensive of modern prams but they offer great variety to adapt as your baby grows up. You have one basic set of wheels into which you can first sit a Group 0/0+ car seat. However, the pushchair is also suitable from birth and the baby can be positioned in a safe, flat position. As your baby grows, you can position the pushchair in a gradually more upright position.

Two-in-one combination prams

By adapting the footrest and the head of the pushchair, you can turn this pushchair into a pram. On some two-in-ones, you can even use the 'pram' position as a carrycot. Once your baby has outgrown the pram, it converts into a pushchair that can either face you or where you are going.

Three-in-one combination prams

A separate carrycot fits into the wheel frame and this can, of course, be used as a first cot. When your baby is big enough, you can use the pushchair attachment as a reclining seat or mini pram. As your baby grows you can then position the pushchair so that it is upright (on some combinations you can choose which way round you put the chair).

Easiriders

These are compact pushchairs that fold flat for storage and popping into a car boot with ease. Despite their small size, they are perfectly safe for newborn babies.

Strollers or buggies

Very lightweight, these are distinguishable from other pushchairs because they have an umbrella-fold, great if you are going to use public transport a lot. However, always check from which age a manufacturer recommends use. Some are suitable from three months but many recommend six months. You certainly shouldn't put a newborn in one of these.

Twin and tandem pushchairs

You don't have to have twins to need one of these. If you have a toddler and a baby, consider buying a twin pushchair which can allow the two seats to be used independently. Twin pushchairs are usually defined as pushchairs where the two

Never allow your baby or toddler to travel in a pram, pushchair or car seat without being correctly restrained. Even if you are not putting your baby in a moving vehicle, it is dangerous if your baby is not securely held in his pram or pushchair.

babies travel side-by-side. A tandem has one child travelling at the front (usually the toddler) and the other reclining at the back (check that it is suitable for a newborn).

All-terrain pushchairs
These are specifically designed to cope with rougher terrain and have much bigger wheels (usually pneumatic) than traditional pushchairs. The whole vehicle is designed to be tougher and more weatherproof than other sorts of prams and pushchairs.

However, some all-terrains are available as a travel system, others are available as a twin option and many are suitable for newborns.

Pram and pushchair accessories

Some top-of-the-range pushchairs and prams may come complete with a range of accessories. Check what is available and whether it is an extra when you are making that all-important decision about which travel option you are going to buy. Think about whether you will need any (or maybe all) of the following things for you and your baby's comfort and amusement.

Raincover
This is probably an essential item, but it should never to be left over your baby indoors or in a shopping centre. You should also keep it well out of your baby's way if it is very sunny, otherwise your baby could overheat.

Weathercosy
A kind of bag that your baby sits in to keep warm. Great for protecting your baby but do be careful not to overdress your baby and cause overheating. Always remove a weathercosy when you are in a shopping centre.

Sunshield or parasol
These will keep the sun from harming your baby. A good parasol should be able to be tilted and moved so that it can be repositioned according to the direction of the sun.

> Be careful about how much shopping and other paraphernalia that you hang from the handles of your pushchair or pram. If your baby is very young or very small, you could tip the vehicle if the extras you are carrying are heavier than he is. Also, bear in mind that if you remove your baby from the vehicle before you take the shopping off, the thing will crash over anyway.

Toys and books
These come in a number of forms but all of them attach to the pram or pushchair in some way. Always check what age they are suitable for and use accordingly. Never position toys so that they are so close to your baby he goes cross-eyed or so that the toy bumps into his face.

Shopping basket
Essential to make your life easier. Some are solid trays that fix beneath the seat (only suitable for pushchairs and prams that fold flat), others are made of soft net and can be positioned either beneath the seat or behind it.

Toddler board
Very handy if you have a small pushchair or stroller and you need to transport a toddler who sometimes walks independently, sometimes doesn't. The board attaches to the back of the chair, near the wheels, and the toddler simply steps on. The toddler will have to hold on to the handles of the chair though. Make sure that the toddler board is compatible with any pushchair or stroller that you have – remember that it either needs to be able to be easily removed or to fold up with the pushchair.

Baby carriers
Baby carriers or slings are a great way to take your baby along to almost anywhere you want to go. If your newborn baby

won't settle or if you need to take the dog for a walk, simple pop your baby in a sling and get on with it. With your baby in a sling, you've got your hands free to get on with the housework or zip around the shops or market. Like most baby kit, there are baby carriers to fit all purse ranges, so bear the following points in mind before you make your decision.

- What do you want to use your sling for? If you do a lot of walking or are very active and used to getting out and about, a baby sling might be the perfect way for you to carry on with that lifestyle so it will get a lot of use. If you think you will only want to use a baby sling for the first few weeks or months until your baby weighs a certain size, then it may be worth either borrowing a sling or buying a smaller sling that is designed for use only up until about 12 months.

- Check to see what age group the manufacturer recommends as suitable for the sling.
- A good sling should have padded leg holes and good padded support for your baby's head.
- Try the sling for comfort and size before you buy. If the nursery store doesn't have a 'dummy' baby for you to try, ask if you can use a large teddy-bear (or take one with you) to try out in the sling. You want to check the sling for ease of use and also for comfort. Remember that any sling will take a few attempts to get the hang of – but if it is uncomfortable for you it's no good.

While a baby carrier is a great way to settle a fretful baby, don't let your baby take advantage of you. It just isn't practical to carry a baby around all the time (and it won't help your sanity either) and your baby needs to learn to spend some time on their own. So, don't feel you've got to pop your baby into a sling every time he cries.

- If you think you will use the sling for some time, check which slings can be used in a variety of ways. A newborn baby is best positioned facing you but, as your baby becomes more aware of his surroundings and his head gets stronger, he will want to see where he is going and travel facing the front. Some slings can be used with the baby positioned on the front (facing both ways) and can then convert to carrying an older toddler on your back.

- If you are going to use the sling for longer walks, make sure that the sling offers proper support for your baby's pelvis.
- Will you and your partner take it in turns to use the sling? If so, look for a sling that easily adapts to fit the wearer each time it is used. If you have to refit lots of buckles and hooks to make the perfect fit, you might find it tedious.
- Is the sling machine washable? If it isn't, is it practical?
- If your baby is going to have to travel on the outside of your clothing during the autumn and winter months, is there a raincape that attaches to provide extra weather protection for your baby?

- Some very traditional slings can even carry twins.
- Some slings require you to position the baby before you put the sling on. Others, you have to get comfy and then pop your baby into the seat. You'll only work out which is more practical for you once you've tried various slings in the shop.
- Once you've got a strong toddler, you may prefer to buy a rigid-framed baby carrier specifically designed for proper all weather use. Again, this should provide support for your toddler and either have a proper harness attached or fixings for you to fix one to. Make sure that there is sufficient padding to protect your own shoulders, back and waist. Basically, if a baby carrier is properly designed and fitted, even a heavy toddler should not hurt your back or feel like a strain is being made.

Chapter 10
Playing

All babies need toys to help them develop, to amuse them and to stimulate them. A newborn baby may not be able to focus or see great distances, but still need things to keep her busy. Safety is always crucial in decision making.

Toys
Some toys are suitable for newborn babies, others from three months – always check the manufacturer's guidelines as some toys may not actually be safe for smaller babies or once a baby becomes more mobile.

Rattles
Wrist rattles can be safely secured to a newborn baby's wrist. You will be surprised how quickly a baby realises that she is

responsible for making the noise. Hand-held rattles are available for older babies, as are harder teething rattles.

Soft toys

There is an enormous variety of these available and your baby will no doubt be given a great deal of them in the first two years of her life. But be warned: only allow your baby to play with a soft toy if the label clearly states that it reaches BSI or ECE standards and that it is suitable for her age. Some soft toys may have clothes or bows which could be pulled off by a very young baby. Also, most toys go into a small baby's mouth and small parts could be a choking hazard.

Mobiles

These provide stimulating images for your baby to watch and can be hung above your usual nappy changing area or perhaps above your baby's cot.

Books

You can read to your baby from birth and there are special board books suitable for just those first few weeks or months. Choose books made of fabric that are soft and tactile – some will make noises when they are rubbed, others will feel different as they are stroked – for very young babies. As your baby gets older, you can use board books.

Baby gyms and activity centres

These can be ideal for your baby to lie under from birth. Your baby lies on a mat with an arch from which toys are suspended above her head. Some can be folded up into a bag so that you can take them with you when you are visiting friends. Always check that the toys are securely attached before you allow your baby to play. An activity centre has reached its limitations once your baby can pull herself up – this is the moment when you should find another way for your baby to play that is safer.

> It is dangerous to leave your baby alone with her toys. Babies need watching at all times.

Playmats

These are basically flat activity centres. Some are quite simple and are covered with bright pictures and merely provide a hygienic area for your baby to lie and play with other toys. Others are designed for your baby to play once she is able to lie on her tummy and push herself up: they have toys and baby mirrors for your baby to explore. You can also buy circular mats that have soft raised sides that provide a 'nest' for your baby.

Balls
A ball is a simple toy that offers hours of amusement. Available as soft scrunchable and chewable fabric balls or soft non-toxic plastic, baby balls make noises, light up and roll away – motivating your baby to get mobile and give chase.

Blocks
Another simple and traditional toy, there are soft blocks, wooden blocks and PVC-covered blocks. Not only will your younger baby spend happy times looking at the pictures and shaking them to make sounds, but your older baby will also begin to have fun stacking them and then knocking them down.

Always make sure that any toys you give your baby conform to BSI and ECE standards. It's also preferable if toys can be machine-washed (if they are made of fabric) or wiped clean (if they are PVC-coated).

Playpens

There will be times when you need to know that your baby is safe and secure when she is playing and you feel that you can't have eyes in the back of your head. This could be because you have a boisterous and mobile toddler tearing around the house or perhaps because you have pets. A playpen could provide the answer.

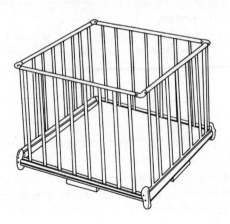

Even a secure environment like a playpen is not an excuse for a baby to be left unattended. Always keep an eye on your baby and make sure that she is safe.

- Remember that some travel cots can also be used as a playpen. So you could save money and double up.
- Some playpens have a traditional pine or painted frame. While these may be more fitting with your décor, you may find that they take up more space in your home. It may be better to ensure that the playpen can be folded flat when it's not in use.
- Traditional playpens have sides constructed of wooden bars – make sure that these are not wide enough for your baby to poke (and perhaps wedge) her head through or your pet to poke its nose through.
- Check that there is a removable play pad for your baby to lie on. Ideally this should be PVC-coated so that it can be wiped clean.
- The sides of the playpen should be high enough so that an older baby who can pull herself up into a standing position cannot climb over.
- Some playpens have sides made of mesh or net providing a soft environment for play.
- A playpen could make a secure play area for a young baby if you are planning a beach holiday. In which case, make sure that the playpen you buy is easily wipeable and can also be easily transported.

Baby bouncers and chairs

Even a very young baby is going to want variety in her play. While she will enjoy playing on her activity mat, it is stimulating for your baby to look around at her environment. A baby chair or bouncer can offer a secure place from which to do this.

Baby bouncers

Baby bouncers (sometimes called bouncing cradles) are lightweight and provide a simple chair that your baby can sit in. Once they are secured with the harness, your baby's own movements will create a gentle bouncing movement.

> Some bouncers are available that can be attached to a door frame. These have a spring mechanism and, once your baby is secured into the soft fabric seat, they use their own feet to bounce and spring. Great fun – but very much only for a limited time of up to 20 minutes. Always make sure that the bouncer is securely attached to the door frame before use.

- Check that there is a headhugger to offer the necessary support for a newborn baby.
- You can attach a bar or arch of toys to provide extra stimulation for your baby.
- It's best if the fabric cover can be removed for machine-washing.

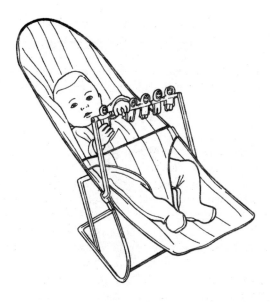

- Some bouncers fold flat for storage when not in use, but not all of them. If space is an issue, check this before you buy.
- If the bouncer does fold flat, it could be useful for taking to grandparents' homes or on holiday.
- Check the recommended maximum age or weight for the bouncer. It is dangerous for a bigger baby to be in a bouncer and babies that have started to pull themselves up could also cause themselves harm.

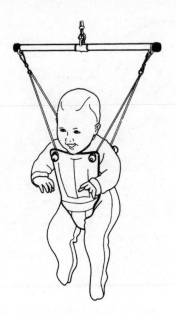

Never leave your baby for long periods of time in a baby bouncer or chair. To ensure maximum safety, position the chair in a secure position on the floor, checking that the spot is draught-free. It is dangerous to position a chair or bouncer on a high table or on a sofa as your baby could rock or bounce themselves off.

Baby chairs

Baby chairs can offer multi-position seats, including a full recline position. Most chairs also offer the option of a rocking or fixed position.

- Ensure that there is a proper harness for your baby to be secured into.
- As with a bouncer, a head hugger is best for ensuring a newborn baby has proper support.

- You may prefer a baby chair that can be folded flat for storage.
- Check that the cover can be removed for machine-washing.
- Carrying handles need to be strong and securely attached.
- You will need to check the maximum age and weight for the chair; once your baby exceeds this, the chair will no longer be safe and suitable.

- Remember that some high-chairs can be used as baby chairs and may offer a swing position as well.
- Some swinging baby chairs are battery powered and can be set to rock your baby automatically. This could be handy if you have a secure and large enough kitchen to position your baby to rock while you clear up.

A baby chair is not a substitute for a car seat and should never be used as one.

Baby-walkers

These have had quite a controversial history. Originally, it was thought that baby-walkers could assist a baby in learning to walk. Now it is recognised that this is not true – indeed if a baby can already walk or get themselves about without assistance, a baby-walker could in fact slow down her desire to get moving under her own steam. Baby-walkers have also had a bad press because some of the older walkers were easily tipped allowing a baby to become trapped. If you are considering a baby-walker bear in mind the following.

- A safe baby-walker should always have eight swivel wheels.
- The seat should be deep enough to allow your baby to sit firmly and securely into it so that her upper body cannot tip the walker over if she leans.
- There should be a bumper bar around the wheels to provide stability.

- You should never leave your baby unattended in a baby-walker.
- The maximum recommended time for playing in a baby-walker is 20 minutes.
- Baby-walkers are only suitable for babies who can secure their own heads into an upright position.
- Be cautious of hazards in the area that your baby will be in: no stairs without stairgates, no coffee tables, no open fires (not even ones with fireguards), and, preferably, no other children running around.
- The baby-walker should be easy to wipe clean – as should any activity toys that come attached to it.

Baby-walkers are not cheap and, bearing in mind the maximum recommended play is 20 minutes, it may seem an expensive piece of play equipment.

Chapter 11
Health and Safety in and around the Home

You need to be aware of safety as soon as your baby is born. It is going to be a long time before you can leave your child unattended while he is awake for any real period of time. Once your baby is mobile, making sure he is safe is a real responsibility, but there are a number of things that you can do to make your house a safer environment.

- Remember that your baby is learning by exploring all the time. So the fact that he couldn't roll one day could change by the next morning and make it unsafe for him to be left on your bed while you sit at the dressing table. Don't wait for an accident to happen before you try to prevent it.

- It's not such a stupid idea to get down on your hands and knees and try to imagine what your home and furniture looks like from your baby's eye level. The edge of a table cloth, when seen from down at carpet level, can look very appealing to tug on.

- If you have any glass doors or a conservatory, the only type of glass that should be fitted is safety glass. No other glass is safe.

- Never drink a hot drink while your baby is on your lap. If your baby makes any unexpected movements and jerks you or your drink, the hot liquid could easily spill on to the baby and cause a serious burn. Even if the drink has been in the cup for 10 or more minutes, it will still be hot enough to cause considerable harm to your baby's delicate skin.
- Fit your kettle with a curly flex. That way the flex will be short enough to be kept away from your inquisitive toddler.
- Keep all pan handles tucked towards the back of the cooker and make sure that they never hang over the front. Even a quite mature toddler who has been repeatedly warned about hot things may be tempted to try to pull themselves up by the handle that they are looking at from below.
- Ask your health visitor for advice about safety in the home. She will also be able to tell you where you can attend a first aid course.
- If you attend a first aid course, or have done in the past, make sure that you attend regular refresher courses to keep your skills up-to-date.
- Your baby or toddler has to learn to respect his home and the things in it. But be realistic – a display of beautiful china objects on a low shelf will probably be hard to resist for any child.
- Learn with your child. As he develops, he will quite possibly not be remotely interested in some potential hazards but may well be fascinated with other things. Be consistent – if you

don't want your baby to play with the video machine, don't be lazy and weaken by not reprimanding them on a busy afternoon. You will only confuse him.

If you leave your child with a babysitter, make sure he or she knows the name and telephone number of your doctor. Also leave the telephone number of where you are going to be – if possible a mobile phone number. It may sound silly, but never assume that they know your actual address, simply because they can find their way to your home. Leave a note of this – name or number of your house and the street that it is in as well as the postcode – next to the phone as it may be needed in an emergency. If you live in a remote or rural location, it may be a good idea to keep the Ordnance Survey reference number near your phone to assist the emergency services in finding you.

Safety gadgets

There are a number of gadgets that you can buy to help you keep your baby from danger. But remember that they will only be worth buying if you use them properly.

Fireguards

Protect your child from any open fires by fitting a proper nursery fireguard. This is a guard that will completely box in any open fire. Make sure that you fit it according to the manufacturer's instructions. This should include a way to fix it on hooks to prevent your baby from being able to pull it towards himself. A flat fireguard that simply gets positioned in front of the fire is not good enough once your baby is mobile.

Locks

There will be some doors that you want to keep permanently locked to ensure that your baby cannot open them. This can be done easily with a key but could be irritating to any adults who need to get in and out of the door on a regular basis. The answer is to fit child-proof locks and latches. There are a number of these available: some are designed specifically for kitchen cupboards, others are specially for fitting on to kitchen appliances. Look around your kitchen and decide what needs

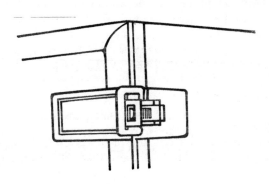

securing: base units, the fridge, the freezer, the oven door, possibly your washing-machine. Now think about the bathroom and any separate loos: some children think it is great fun to drop things into the lavatory and watch the splash, others could open the lid, take a good look in and then lose their balance, thus tumbling in. Consider fixing a catch on the outside of the door to prevent your toddler from entering or, perhaps more practical, fix a specially designed lock on the loo seat itself.

Window catches

Even a downstairs window can be dangerous to small children – if they manage to climb on to the windowsill, a drop of only a foot or two could cause physical damage. Even if the fall doesn't stop them, a toddler could then make his way into the great outdoors. Ensure that all windows have safety locks (some PVC-U windows may already have integral locks): they are available for both hinged and sash windows and can be used even when the window if slightly open. In some circumstances, it may be necessary to fit grilles to ensure safety.

Glass safety film

As it says on page 164, the only safe glass is safety glass. But, glass safety film, if properly applied, can convert ordinary glass to prevent it from shattering in the event of an accident.

Stairgates

You need to prevent your baby from getting up and down the stairs so it will probably be necessary to fit a stairgate on the landing as well as in the hall. Remember that a stairgate will only be safe if it is properly secured to the wall, so follow the manufacturer's instructions. Check that the gate is suitable for the position that you want to fix it to. A gate that you have to climb over will be tedious to use and possibly dangerous if you have a baby in your arms. Most have an opening section or

allow you to open the entire gate on a hinge. However, if only
the central section opens, decide whether the gap is going to be
wide enough for you to use safely. Also, there may be a step
beneath the opening – if this is high it could be a trip hazard.
You can buy wooden gates which may be more in keeping with
your décor. Others are white painted metal or made of a fabric
mesh (which of course provide a softer land if bumped into).
Some gates are also designed to be portable – which could be
handy if you need to visit granny. The most expensive gates are
fitted with alarms that let you know if they have been opened.
Of course, these will only be effective if you remember to
change the batteries on a regular basis.

Socket guards and covers

Most toddlers cannot resist the temptation to poke their finger
or part of a toy (or maybe even some food) into a hole – so
don't wait to see if your toddler wants to do this with a socket.
Socket covers fix simply and quickly into the pin holes of the
socket, preventing anything else from being pushed in. Socket
guards need to be fitted to the socket box (you'll need to switch
off the electricity to do this) and, once they are, they allow the
socket to be used without the toddler tampering with it.
Obviously, you will be discouraging your toddler from playing
with sockets, but a socket guard will protect electrical items on
timers from being switched off.

Pram and cot nets

If you have a cat, you will soon discover that they are always tempted to climb into the cot to snuggle up with baby. There is not only a hygiene issue here but, as cats naturally gravitate to warm things, they usually want to curl up on the baby – potentially dangerous if the cat is large or it lays near a baby's face. Fitting a net over your cot (and the pram if you leave your baby to sleep in the pram in the garden on a warm day) will put the cat off and allow your baby to sleep in peace. A net will also protect your baby from insects.

Thermometers

Already mentioned on pages 69 and 79, these will make sure that you don't put your baby in a bath that is dangerously hot or even too cold. In the nursery, they will also guide you as to the amount of clothing and bed-linen your baby needs.

Door stoppers

Nasty accidents can happen when small fingers get trapped in a door hinge or as a door closes. If a door is fitted near a radiator, a baby could also get trapped between the door and the hot radiator if the door closes on them. Take a good look around your house and work out which doors would be safer left open permanently with the benefit of a doorstop or a catch which holds the door against the wall. You can use a traditional doorstop or invest in a child-safe one. In other cases, it may be more appropriate to fit simple cushion device that clips around the door and prevents the door from slamming shut on fingers.

Corner protectors and cushions

These slip and clip on to the corners of tables and the edges of work surfaces and soften the blow if a baby or toddler bumps into them.

Cooker and hob guards

Although you should always keep pan handles out of a child's reach, a cooker guard fits to the front of your cooker or hob and prevents your toddler from touching. Some guards tilt out but others fix in a flat upright position; some protect only the front of the hob, others around the front and both sides. Do check carefully, though, to see if the guard is compatible with your model of cooker.

Flex grabbers

Try to fit as many surface-dwelling appliances with curly flex as is practical. But equipment such as computers, stereos, videos and televisions usually require a number of sockets and wires. Keep these neat and protected from small prying fingers by clipping them into a flex cover or grabber.

Video cover

Small children love posting things and a video machine makes a great postbox. Either position your video machine in a place that toddlers can't reach or fit a video cover or guard that keeps the video slot out of reach.

Bath mat
Already mentioned on page 79, this can prevent all members of the family from slipping in the bath. You can also obtain smaller mats for showers.

Bed guards
These are designed to fit on to the side of the bed to prevent toddlers and young children from falling out of their first bed. Make sure that it is easy to fold down to allow the child to get safely in and out of the bed, as well as for storytime and when you need to change the bed linen.

Rug grippers
These attach very simply to the bottom of a rug or unfitted carpet to stop it from slipping on a shiny floor and causing a trip or slip hazard.

Night lights
Not a safety item as such but, because they provide a gentle but reassuring light in either a bedroom, hall or landing, they can prevent a baby or child from panicking in the dark.

> If you use a baby monitor, make sure that each of the two units is in a safe place away from water and heat. Also ensure that either unit is not placed in a position where it can be tampered with or a toddler can pull it down by the flex. Remember that a toddler may want to 'help' you by 'talking' to their younger sibling via the adult monitor.

Fire safety

If you have an open or gas fire, make sure that you always keep matches well out of reach of children and babies. Then make sure that you put an appropriate guard in front of the fire (see page 166–7). But your home is not only vulnerable from fires that are intended to keep you warm, of course. Consider the following to make your home and family as safe and protected from fire as you can.

> Teach your children their name and address as early as you possibly can. Then teach them how to dial 999 and give these details. Even very young children can help to save lives in this way.

- Never overload sockets.
- Ask an electrician to check the wiring in your house. Old or bad wiring can be lethal.

- Fit smoke alarms both upstairs and downstairs and make sure that the batteries are regularly replaced. Check that the alarms are in working order on a regular basis.
- Never leave a burning candle unattended or near curtains or other soft furnishings.
- Always make sure that cigarettes are properly extinguished.
- Work out your escape route in the event of a fire. Remember: fires don't just happen at night – so determine the quickest and safest route that you would follow to get out of the house whether you are upstairs or down.
- Don't forget that you may not be able to get down the stairs during a fire. Make sure that there is a window that you can use as your fire escape.
- You may want to buy a rope ladder which you can keep under the bed. This can be dropped from a window and used as a fire escape.
- Keep keys for window and door locks near to them so that you can use them quickly.
- It's obviously sensible to lock your front and back doors at night, but make sure that any keys are close to them. If they aren't and there is a fire, you will be locked in.
- Smoke inhalation causes as much harm as fire. If you are caught in a fire, close as many doors as possible to prevent the fire from spreading. Then cover the base of the door with a sheet, blanket or towel (preferably damp) to prevent the smoke from entering the room while you wait for help.

Smoking is not only dangerous to your own health, but it also harms your unborn baby and any other babies and children you live with. Your midwife, health visitor or doctor will be able to give you help and advice to help you and your partner stop smoking. If you must still smoke, NEVER smoke in the same room as your baby or children – they will have no choice but to smoke your cigarettes passively, putting them at risk of breathing and chest problems, as well as cancer. Cigarettes also start fires.

- Never leave a pan with hot fat unattended – even if you just want to answer the phone.
- Keep a fire blanket in an easily accessible place in your kitchen and make sure that you read the instructions before you ever have to use it.
- If a fat pan catches fire, never pour water over it. Cover it with a fire blanket or a towel.
- If another pan catches fire, cover it with a fire blanket or a damp tea towel.
- Make sure that you only buy furniture and soft furnishings that comply with current fire hazard precautions. Check the swing ticket that will be hanging from such items in the shop or showroom. If furnishing and fabric don't comply with safety standards, don't buy them.

- Double glazing is almost impossible to break. If you already have double glazed windows in your home, make sure that every bedroom has a window that can be easily opened and used as an escape route in a fire. If you are about to have double glazing fitted, have this done by a reputable builder or company – and make sure that they bear fire escapes in mind when windows are fitted. If they don't automatically do this and you have to ask them about it, should you be using such a company anyway?

Your first aid kit and baby medicine cabinet

Every home should have a first aid kit and if yours hasn't, visit a chemist immediately and purchase one. It's probably a good idea to have a kit in your car as well. Hopefully, your newborn baby or toddler won't be having an accident, but there are a few basic items that are only sensible to have to hand in every home.

Gripe water

All babies get trapped wind at times and some get griping pains. Gripe water is usually suitable to use from about four weeks of age (always check the label to make sure). Make sure that it is sugar, colour and alcohol-free.

Colic drops

An alternative to gripe water, these come in a dropper container making it easy to administer. Again, make sure that they are colour, sugar and alcohol-free. They are usually suitable to use from birth.

Infant paracetamol

This can be given for fast relief from pain and fever; most health visitors recommend giving babies infant paracetamol when they have their first inoculations. Only for babies over three months of age. Check that the formula is colour, sugar and alcohol-free.

Infant cough and cold relief

This is available as an over-the-counter medicine. However, you must check with the pharmacist to see if it is recommended for babies.

Always keep medicines out of reach of children. Only buy medication that comes in a child-proof container – if medicine is being dispensed, make sure that your pharmacist takes this into account. Keep medicine in a lockable medicine cabinet – and make sure that you keep any key for it safely away from your children.

Menthol rubs

These are intended for use as a topical application to help clear congestion and assist breathing during a cold. Check the manufacturer's instructions as to what age it is recommended for as some rubs are quite strong, and may be too strong for babies under three or six months.

Menthol drops
Designed to be dropped on to your baby's bed-linen to assist breathing and congestion when they have a cold, these are great for adults, too. With a very young baby, you should put the drops on to a hanky or muslin square that you tie from the cot. They are probably suitable for use from three months, but check the manufacturer's guidelines.

Easy-breathe bath additive
Again, this will help your baby when he has a cold, but might not be suitable for use until your baby is six months old.

Infant medicine spoon
Most medicine will be supplied with one of these or your pharmacist will check if you need one. A double-ended spoon should have a 5ml bowl at one end and a 2.5ml measure at the other to allow the accurate dosage to be given.

Medicine syringe
Some babies and toddlers won't take medicine from a spoon. If this is the case, ask your pharmacist for a medicine syringe. This can be placed into the neck of the bottle and you simply 'draw'

the medicine up to the prescribed dosage. Then pop the syringe into your child's mouth and gently push the medicine in.

Thermometer

There are many thermometers on the market and these range considerably in price. A simple glass thermometer is perfectly good, but is not easy to use on a wriggling infant who doesn't understand about keeping it under his tongue for a short while. He could also bite on the glass – which is obviously not desirable. The simplest infant thermometer is a forehead strip. You simply place this across your child's forehead and it quickly displays his temperature – usually indicating by colour as well as a given reading. Digital thermometers can be safely used in an infant's mouth or also in the armpit. Ear thermometers are expensive but claim to give a reading in only one second and are suitable for use by the whole family as they come complete with disposable ear pieces.

> It's a good idea to keep a record of the 'normal' temperature of all members of your family. ('Normal' can vary between different people.) Keep this in the same place as your thermometer and you will instantly be able to know if a reading taken when your child is sick indicates a fever. If you are in doubt about taking a temperature reading, or need advice about what is normal for your children, ask your doctor or health visitor for advice.

Useful Websites

Pregnancy and new motherhood is a time when you may not have either the time or the energy to traipse around the shops to look for goods or advice. Make the most of the internet to trace the best bargains, track down information, and to get organised.

Remember that many websites are commercial and may not offer impartial advice. Websites are not substitutes for proper medical care and health advice from your GP, midwife or health visitor.

Baby clothes

www.jojomamanbebe.co.uk
www.ukparents.co.uk
www.mothercare.com
www.hopscotchmailorder.co.uk
www.letterbox.uk.com
www.sleepcozy.com
www.bebamour.co.uk
www.kiddycarebabybags.com
www.grobag.co.uk
www.snugasabug.co.uk
www.grobag.co.uk
www.bonnenuit.co.uk
www.safetysleeper.com
www.babiesrus.co.uk

Birth announcements

www.announceit.co.uk
www.riancraft.co.uk
www.telltheworld.co.uk

Food and nutrition

www.hipp.co.uk
www.babyorganix.co.uk
www.milupa.co.uk
www.pronatal.co.uk

www.tesco.com
www.pregnacare.com
www.beamingbaby.com
www.asda.co.uk
www.sainsburystoyou.co.uk
www.vitabiotics.co.uk
www.foe.co.uk

Health and beauty advice

www.netdoctor.co.uk
www.patients.co.uk
www.nhsdirect.nhs.uk
www.askyourpharmacist.co.uk
www.wellbeing.com
www.spd-uk.org
www.maternalbliss.com
www.thesanctuary.co.uk
www.healthfarms.co.uk
www.oilatum.co.uk
www.sudocrem.bounty.com
www.loveyourskin.co.uk
www.ethosbaby.com
www.beamingbaby.com
www.sids.org.uk
www.aventbaby.com
www.pronatal.co.uk

www.vitabiotics.com
www.pregnacare.com

Maternity clothes
www.jojomamanbebe.co.uk
www.beforebaby.com
www.bloomingmarvellous.co.uk
www.formes.com
www.bumpstart.co.uk
www.mothercare.com
www.mothernaturebras.co.uk
www.preciouscargo.co.uk

Mother and baby care products
www.nctpregnancyandbabycare.com
www.ce.philips.com/babycare
www.aventbaby.com
www.mothercare.com
www.caboodlebags.co.uk
www.ethosbaby.com
www.beamingbaby.com
www.babycalm.com
www.waterbirth.co.uk
www.babiesrus.co.uk
www.safetysleeper.com

www.zorbit.co.uk
www.pregnacare.com

Nappies
www.pampers.co.uk
www.huggiesclub.com
www.cuddlebabes.co.uk
www.earthlets.co.uk
www.bambino.co.uk
www.cottonbottoms.co.uk
www.naturallynappies.co.uk
www.snugglenaps.co.uk
www.yummiesnappies.co.uk
www.phpbaby.com

Out and about (pushchairs, car seats, and carriers)
www.mountainbuggy.com
www.kidsense.co.uk
www.britax.co.uk
www.cheekyrascals.co.uk
www.bush-baby.com
www.practicalpushchairs.co.uk
www.mothercare.com
www.babiesrus.co.uk

www.outnabout-atp.co.uk
www.babybackpacs.co.uk
www.allterrain.co.uk
www.caboodlebags.co.uk
www.earthlets.co.uk

Toys and gifts
www.mothercare.com
www.babiesrus.com
www.wowtoys.co.uk
www.ethosbaby.com
www.flairplc.co.uk
www.goshshop.co.uk
www.babygem.com
www.letterbox.uk.com
www.orchardtoys.com
www.fisher-price.com/uk

Index